At Home Café

Gatherings for Family and Friends

At Home Café
Gatherings for Family and Friends

Helen Puckett DeFrance

with Carol Puckett • Foreword by Art Smith

RODALE

In memory of my beloved grandmother Helen Todd,
who taught me the simple joys of cooking.

Rodale books may be purchased for business or promotional use or for special sales. For information, please write to:
Special Markets Department, Rodale, Inc., 733 Third Avenue, New York, NY 10017

Printed in China
Rodale Inc. makes every effort to use acid-free ∞, recycled paper ♻.

Recipe on page 114 is from *Foster's Market Cookbook* by Sara Foster © 2002 by Sara Foster.
Used by permission of Random House, Inc.

Photographs on pages 5, 15, 25, 35, 38, 41, 49, 59, 65, 77, 83, 91, 99, 110, 121, 125, 135,
145, 154, 169, 181, 187, 193, 196, 200 © Mitch Mandel/Rodale Images; pages i, xii, 10, 20, 30, 44, 60, 72,
86, 94, 104, 116, 130, 140, 150, 160, 174, 188 © Thomas MacDonald/Rodale Images; page 211, courtesy of the author

Book design by Christina Gaugler

Library of Congress Cataloging-in-Publication Data

DeFrance, Helen Puckett.
    At home café : gatherings for family and friends : 125 all new crowd-pleasing dishes tested by Viking Cooking School /
Helen Puckett DeFrance with Carol Puckett ; foreword by Art Smith.
        p.   cm.
Includes index.
ISBN-13 978–1–59486–843–6 hardcover
ISBN-10 1–59486–843–3 hardcover
1. Entertaining.   2. Cookery.   3. Menus.   I. Puckett, Carol.   II. Viking Cooking School.   III. Title.
TX731.D4477 2008
642'.4—dc22   2008021891

Distributed to the trade by Macmillan

2   4   6   8   10   9   7   5   3   hardcover

We inspire and enable people to improve their lives and the world around them
For more of our products visit **rodalestore.com** or call 800-848-4735

Contents

Thank You

A heartfelt thanks to my parents, Ben and Dorothy Puckett, who taught me to believe I could do whatever I wanted to do, and who have patiently supported me in chasing my dreams. I am forever grateful to my mother, who taught me her gracious style of entertaining and love of beautiful things.

Without my sister, Carol, this book would not have been possible. Not only did she help make this dream a reality—she also graciously agreed to write the prose, an arduous task she performed on weekends and late nights after long days at her "real" job as president of the Viking Hospitality Group.

And to my brothers, Richard, Ben, John, and Todd, who have always supported me and stood by me in all of my adventures, this one being the most challenging. To their families for their continued love, encouragement, and delicious recipes.

The good folks at Regal Literary deserve a lifetime supply of pound cakes and pies. I thank my agents, Bess Reed Currence and Michael Psaltis: Bess for her patience, support, and hand-holding—not to mention the sage advice and recipes from her husband, award-winning chef John Currence of City Grocery in Oxford, Mississippi, who contributed an entire chapter of recipes to this book; and Michael for his wisdom and confidence in me as he and Bess guided me through my first solo writing endeavor.

My sincere thanks goes to Rodale's Liz Perl, who believed in my vision and made the leap to publish this book. And to Marya Dalrymple, the most amazing editor, who has worked diligently and patiently with me to make this the best book possible, even during seemingly impossible deadlines. A very special thanks also goes to Shea Zukowski, along with Chris Gaugler and the entire team at Rodale, whose meticulous attention to every detail is evident in the final product.

I am truly grateful to Fred and Margaret Carl, and the Viking Range Corporation, especially Joe

Sherman, who believed in this book enough to take on the task of testing the recipes. His amazing team at the Viking Cooking School, headed by Bob Pavy, magically made it all happen.

And to Martha Stewart who introduced me to a national audience by inviting me to be her guest on *The Martha Stewart Show*.

I will be forever grateful to my dear friend and mentor Kreis Beall, who has continued to believe in me, encourage me, and challenge me. And to Sam and Mary Celeste Beall and the entire team at the luxurious Blackberry Farm resort for their continued support and belief in my kids' cooking programs. To Susan Hill for accepting the task of being my "Mississippi editor" and to Rachel Shows for her endless hours of typing and retyping. To Willie Mae Winters for keeping my aprons ironed and looking after my son, Martin, and me.

I also want to acknowledge my wonderful book group who served as testers and critics for my recipes—the good and not-so-good. Thank you Lady Bettye, Ed, Betty, John, Ann, Jane, Ruth, Margie, Tim, Pat, Rebecca, and Deaver for your steadfastness and willingness to participate in this adventure. Thank you as well to my friend Marsha for being a continuous sounding board and support.

I am eternally grateful to Art Smith for his experience and wisdom. Thanks also to John T. Edge of the Southern Foodways Alliance for introducing me to the most fabulous agents around and for his support of my kids' cooking program.

And to my cooking students and student assistants Clara Frances, Cameron, Sam, Rose, Sylvie, William, Duncan, Mary Christopher, Kali, and Kierstin, who not only let me teach them but also kindly allowed me to include their recipes in this book.

Most of all, to my son and favorite cooking partner, Martin.

Foreword

In the culinary universe, there is one area that always shines. And that is food made at home. If you're like me, your fondest memories are of the dishes made by your mother, grandmother, or another family member. For me, food means love, and I believe that there's no better way to show it than by cooking a meal for family and friends in your own kitchen.

Today, sadly, many home kitchens are like little restaurants with parents acting as short-order cooks as they try to satisfy everyone's divergent tastes. Some of us may do this and smile, but for many of us, it's merely exhausting. And the idea of having some great people over for a dinner party, much less a casual a picnic. . . . Who has the time? So how can we change things and recreate the ambiance of kitchens (and dining rooms and backyards) filled with great food and the joys of time spent with those closest to us?

Well, help is here and she's got a southern accent. Helen DeFrance is one of the greatest mothers (and cooks) I know, besides my beloved Addie Mae, of course. Helen has an amazing relationship with her teenage son, Martin, and has passed her love of food and gatherings on to him. Which brings me to a key point: Good parenting helps foster a love of good food in a child, along with the other great lessons of life, of course.

And another point: What's great about recipes from a southern lady like Helen is that she's tried out all of them on her friends before sharing them with you. Whether it's a dinner for 4 or a barbecue for 20, her gracious style is her trademark. There's no doubt in my mind that once you've had a chance to prepare her recipes, you'll quickly gain a reputation for being as fine a host or hostess as she is. You'll learn from her easy-to-follow recipes as she takes you step-by-step through the perfect shrimp and grits or the ultimate spaghetti pie (Mother Addie Mae, take note of this recipe!). And you'll want to share these memorable dishes at wonderful gatherings with your own family and friends.

In life we meet many people, and being a person of great faith, I believe they all come into our lives for a reason. Helen DeFrance came into my life to be my dear friend, and, as luck would have it, one who always leaves me with a freshly baked pound cake and other delicious things. As a single mother, she clearly understands what it's like to face our busy world. But she adds a little sugar to it and shows us that cooking for those we love is a wonderful gift that creates lifelong bonds.

So enter At Home Café, pull up to the table, and select some of Helen's delicious recipes. Then get the whole family together, and some good friends and neighbors too, and cook a meal. But remember, do it with love and laughter, because food cooked without these ingredients surely doesn't taste very good.

—Art Smith

chef, author, and television personality

Introduction

I learned to cook from my grandmother, but I learned to create beautiful and simple dinners from my mother.

When my first book was published, my mother accompanied me on several speaking engagements. She sat patiently in the back of the room and listened to me talk of spending endless hours in the kitchen with my grandmother learning to cook. Finally one day she asked a question that had obviously been weighing on her mind for some time, "Did you learn anything from me?"

My answer went something like this. "Of course I learned from you. I learned everything about entertaining from you. I started helping serve at your dinner parties when I was 10 years old."

Whether she was at the supermarket pushing two carts full of groceries or at a Little League baseball game with a swarm of children around her, well-meaning people engaged my mother in conversations about her large family that invariably ended with the question, "How do you do it all with six kids?" I was always puzzled when someone asked this because she did it so effortlessly. In a recent mother-daughter moment, I asked the old "How did you do it?" question and her answer was very simple. "I did it with a little planning. Every Sunday night, I made out a menu for the week and posted it in the kitchen."

As far back as I can remember, my mother always had a game plan, and she taught me how to play the game. With a game plan, you can create memorable meals from the most casual gathering to the most formal dinner. My mother taught me her love of entertaining and how to create beautiful dinners. She also taught me the importance of the family table. Whether dinner is a simple sandwich for my son, Martin, and me or a feast for a rowdy table of six children, she taught me the importance of sitting down and sharing a meal together.

This book will help you create a simple dinner for your family, a gathering for friends and neighbors, or an elegant dinner party. It will show you how to involve others in the cooking process so that time in the kitchen is not a chore, but an opportunity to spend time with friends and family. Each of us is busy with the endless demands of modern life, but we shouldn't be too busy to enjoy the fun, fellowship, and special moments that cooking and sharing meals together brings.

Recently I traveled to Chicago and spent the afternoon with Art Smith, Oprah Winfrey's longtime executive chef and proprietor of the acclaimed restaurant Table Fifty-Two. Art and I had become fast friends—he sometimes refers to me as his "Mississippi sister." Art and I talked over a cup of coffee about our cookbooks and our passion for teaching kids, then moved on to wine as the afternoon turned to evening. He gave me lots of sage advice and, as I got up to leave, his parting comment was this: "Honey, out of everything that I've told you, the most important advice is to start writing stories." That is what this book is all about. It's a collection of not only delicious recipes but also the stories of the people and places that have been important in my life. It's about my lively and colorful big family. It's about the friends I've met in my travels and those who are part of my everyday life, and all that they bring to the table. There's only one person who could help me write my stories—my sister, Carol. Carol has been writing stories since she was born, and I love the way she weaves a tale. As busy as she is, or as hard as she is working, she always finds the time to do what she loves most, which is to write—just like I find the time to cook with kids, friends, and family.

—Helen DeFrance

CHAPTER 1

Rise and Shine

for 8 guests

As far back as I can remember, my mother would habitually remind me that breakfast is the most important meal of the day. "Start with a good breakfast," she would say, "and you'll have a good day." On school mornings, there was always a hearty, healthy breakfast on the table, and on weekends we dabbled in more exotic fare with the entire family crowded in the small kitchen making pancakes, French toast, or some concoction.

Breakfast is a wonderful time to gather with friends and family and greet the day. Morning gatherings are typically more casual in nature, and guests are hungry and eager to "break the fast" after the previous night's dinner and sleep.

To this day, my mother enjoys entertaining and often has overnight houseguests. They always wake up to a beautiful breakfast served simply, but with great style, on unusual plates or bowls that she has collected through the years. Her guests never fail to appreciate these special touches, and I learned from her many years ago that even the plainest breakfast food—whether a boiled egg or piece of toast—can be elevated by its presentation.

This is one of my favorite breakfast menus because it's so flexible and offers numerous options to adapt the recipes to the ingredients on hand. I often start my cooking classes with this menu. It's a good way to begin the day and get everyone involved in the cooking process. Even a 2-year-old is delighted to help by squeezing the oranges. Fresh fruit and yogurt can be layered with the Blackberry Farmhouse Cereal to make a breakfast parfait; and the "no yeast" sweet rolls are guaranteed to be a hit.

Create your own version of the breakfast burrito by combining leftover cheeses and meats with the eggs and rolling them up in flour tortillas. No breakfast menu in my part of the world would be complete without grits—and these are easy and delicious.

The tasty brown sugar sausage recipe comes from my dear friends the Rupperts in Baltimore. I met this exceptional family several years ago while teaching cooking to their daughters Kali and Kierstin at Blackberry Farm in Walland, Tennessee. We have continued our yearly tradition of spending a holiday at Blackberry Farm and have expanded our visits to meet other times of the year as well. Kali and Kierstin made this breakfast for us during our vacation in the Florida panhandle resort of Seaside.

Helping Hands

Help from the Seasoned Cook

Homemade Sweet Rolls are delicious and fun to make, and are a good task to hand over to a seasoned cook.

Help from the Kids

Kids enjoy wrapping the Brown Sugar Sausages and securing them with toothpicks. Even a 2-year-old will delight in squeezing fresh orange juice.

Brown Sugar Sausages

1 (12-ounce) package bacon

1 (16-ounce) package cocktail smokies

2 cups firmly packed brown sugar

Preheat the oven to 350°F. Line a baking sheet with parchment or foil and top with a wire rack (this allows the sausages to drain and makes them nice and crispy).

Cut the bacon slices into thirds. Wrap each smokie in a piece of bacon and secure with a toothpick.

Place on the rack on the baking sheet and cover with brown sugar.

Bake for 45 minutes, or until the bacon is browned and crisp and the smokies are heated through.

Makes 8 servings

Kitchen Note

- To get ahead, you can wrap the cocktail sausages with the bacon, cover, and refrigerate overnight.

Breakfast Grits

4 cups milk

1 teaspoon salt

¾ cup grits (not quick-cooking)

4 tablespoons unsalted butter

2 cups shredded sharp Cheddar cheese

4 large eggs, separated

¼ to ½ teaspoon cayenne pepper

Preheat the oven to 375°F. Butter a 9- by 13-inch casserole.

Bring milk and salt to a boil in a large heavy saucepan over medium heat.

Pour in grits and simmer, stirring constantly, until thick and perfectly smooth, about 20 minutes.

Add butter, stir, and remove from the heat.

Add cheese, egg yolks, and cayenne, and blend well. Set aside, covered, to thicken but keep warm.

In a large, clean bowl, beat egg whites until stiff but not dry and grainy. Fold into grits mixture.

Pour mixture into the prepared casserole. Bake for 30 to 40 minutes, or until golden brown and firm in the middle.

Makes 8 servings

Sunrise Burritos

12 large eggs

½ cup milk

1 tablespoon unsalted butter

1 (4-ounce) can diced green chiles, drained

Salt and pepper

8 (10-inch) flour tortillas

1½ cups shredded Monterey Jack cheese

Salsa

Sour cream

Whisk eggs and milk in a large bowl until completely combined.

Melt butter in a large skillet over medium-low heat and add eggs. Cook for 5 minutes, stirring frequently.

Stir in chiles. Cook, stirring constantly, until eggs are cooked, 2 to 3 minutes. Season with salt and pepper.

Heat tortillas in a large dry skillet over medium heat.

For each serving, place a tortilla in the center of a plate and spoon one-eighth of the egg mixture down the middle.

Sprinkle cheese over eggs and fold sides of tortillas over eggs to close. Place burritos on individual plates and top each with some salsa and a spoonful of sour cream.

Makes 8 servings

Kitchen Notes

- The cheese may be mixed in while scrambling the eggs. Bacon, sausage, or Canadian bacon may be added to the egg mixture.
- For a crunchier burrito, place a filled tortilla seam side down in a buttered pan and bake in a 350°F oven for 3 to 4 minutes.

Homemade Sweet Rolls

Dough

- 1 cup cottage cheese
- ¾ cup sugar
- 3 large eggs
- ½ cup vegetable oil
- ½ cup milk
- 2 tablespoons baking powder
- 4¼ cups all-purpose flour

Filling

- 2 cups firmly packed brown sugar
- 3 tablespoons ground cinnamon
- ½ cup unsalted butter, melted
- ½ cup honey
- 1 cup raisins or chopped pecans (optional)

Glaze

- 2½ cups confectioners' sugar
- ¼ cup half-and-half
- 1 teaspoon vanilla extract

Preheat the oven to 325°F. Lightly butter or spray the bottom and sides of a 9- by 13-inch baking pan.

To make dough: Place cottage cheese in a blender or food processor and puree until smooth.

Add sugar, eggs, oil, and milk and puree until smooth.

Pour mixture into a large bowl and stir in baking powder.

Add 3½ cups of the flour and stir until mixture forms a dough.

Using your hands, add remaining ¾ cup of flour a little at a time by sprinkling a little over dough and folding dough over to mix it in. Repeat until dough is smooth and not sticky. (You may not need all the flour.)

Sprinkle a thin layer of flour on a flat work surface and roll the dough into a large rectangle, about 20 by 25 inches.

To make filling: Combine brown sugar and cinnamon in a small bowl.

Brush butter over entire surface of the dough.

Drizzle honey over butter, then sprinkle sugar mixture evenly over dough.

If you like, sprinkle raisins or pecans evenly over dough.

Starting on the longer side, carefully roll up dough as tightly as possible.

Using a serrated knife, cut roll into 16 to 20 slices (1¼–1½-inch) with a sawing motion. (If you press down while cutting the dough, it will smash together and lose the "roll" effect.)

Arrange cinnamon rolls in the prepared pan. Bake for 35 to 40 minutes, or until dough pulls apart when you pull up slightly on the center of one of the rolls in the middle of the pan. (If dough stretches, it needs to cook more.)

Run a knife around the edges to loosen the rolls and invert the pan onto a serving platter.

To make glaze: Combine glaze ingredients in a medium bowl and stir until smooth.

Drizzle glaze over tops of rolls.

Makes 16–20 sweet rolls

Kitchen Notes

- Place the baking dish on a baking sheet in case of drips.
- To make the sweet rolls ahead, carefully roll the dough as tightly as possible, wrap in parchment, and refrigerate for up to 1 day. To bake, slice the chilled dough; place it in a greased pan, and bring to room temperature. Follow the baking instructions in the recipe.
- If you have any leftovers, they reheat perfectly in a microwave oven.

Blackberry Farmhouse Cereal

2 cups old-fashioned rolled oats

½ cup sliced almonds

½ cup raw cashews

½ cup shredded coconut

½ cup pecan pieces

¼ cup pine nuts

¼ cup wheat germ

1½ teaspoons sesame seeds

1½ teaspoons walnut oil

Zest of 1 orange

4 tablespoons unsalted butter

1 cup honey

¼ cup apple juice

1 tablespoon firmly packed brown sugar

1 cup assorted dried fruit, diced

Preheat the oven to 200°F. Line a baking sheet with aluminum foil.

In a large bowl, combine oats, almonds, cashews, coconut, pecans, pine nuts, wheat germ, sesame seeds, oil, and orange zest.

Melt butter in a medium skillet over medium heat. Add honey, apple juice, and brown sugar and cook until sugar just dissolves.

Pour honey mixture over oat mixture and toss to coat evenly. Spread oat mixture evenly on the prepared baking sheet.

Bake for 30 minutes, or until crisp (the longer the cereal cooks, the crispier it will become). Let cereal cool on the pan.

Toss cereal with dried fruit.

Enjoy with yogurt or milk or just by itself!

Makes 1¼ quarts

Kitchen Note

● The dry ingredients can be easily assembled ahead of time and stored in an airtight container for up to 3 days until ready to complete the recipe. After baking and cooling, store the cereal in an airtight container.

Breakfast Parfaits

These delicious breakfast parfaits are a tasty way to wake up the senses. They feature Blackberry Farmhouse Cereal, fresh fruit, and vanilla yogurt, with a drizzle of honey over all.

2 cups fresh strawberries

2 pints fresh blackberries, raspberries, or blueberries, or a combination of berries

6 cups lowfat vanilla yogurt

2 cups Blackberry Farmhouse Cereal (opposite)

4 tablespoons honey

Gently wash and dry all of the berries. Hull and cut strawberries into bite-size pieces.

Combine strawberries with fresh berries in a medium bowl.

Spoon a layer of vanilla yogurt into the bottom of each of 8 tall glasses. Add a layer of berries and sprinkle with a layer of Blackberry Farmhouse Cereal. Repeat the layering once or twice, depending on the height of the glasses, ending with a layer of Blackberry Farmhouse Cereal.

Drizzle with honey.

Makes 8 servings

Kitchen Notes

- Use fresh fruit when it's available. Otherwise unsweetened frozen or canned fruit is perfectly acceptable.
- I like to garnish the parfaits with fresh mint from my garden.

CHAPTER 2

Deep South Brunch

for 8 guests

One summer I came home from camp and asked my mother why all the other campers said I talked like I was from the Deep South. She told me to go look out the front door and come back and tell her what I saw. I opened the big front door of our home in Pass Christian, Mississippi, and stared out at the Gulf of Mexico. The realization swept over me like the Gulf breeze through the ancient oak trees in our front yard. I truly lived in the "Deep South" and you couldn't get more Southern than that.

Brunch is a mainstay of entertaining in the South, and we celebrate just about any life event with a brunch. Offering the best of breakfast with the heartier fare of lunch, how can you go wrong? It's the perfect pregame get-together during football season or after-church gathering to commemorate a christening or other special event. It's the ideal lazy morning meal for house parties and a wonderful way to entertain out-of-town guests on the day of a wedding.

The first consideration of most any Deep South brunch is what kind of grits will be served. Grits are typically dressed up for a brunch with cheese and seasonings and serve as the perfect accompaniment for an egg dish. On my family table, you'll usually find Shrimp and Grits. Everyone seems to have their favorite shrimp and grits recipe, and this is the one my youngest brother, Todd, has perfected. In a family that loves to cook and entertain, Todd stands out as the most adventurous among us. Weekends usually find him in the kitchen trying something new and challenging or creating innovative riffs on traditional regional dishes.

He and his wife Rivers have four young children and live in the picturesque waterfront community of Fairhope, Alabama. They avail themselves of all things related to life on the water, from sailing and fishing to cooking the abundance of fresh seafood caught in the Gulf of Mexico and Mobile Bay. Although Rivers is a fine cook herself, the kitchen is Todd's domain. Perhaps as the baby in a family of six children, he learned something different about cooking from each of his older siblings and became the most creative cook of us all.

Canadian bacon or a good country ham complements the grits and eggs, and at Christmas brunch we always serve quail, which my father cooks on the grill—no matter the temperature outside. Sweet rolls or biscuits go well with this menu, as do assorted nut breads. This is the perfect occasion to get out pretty accessories for jams and jellies and set out glass pitchers full of various juices so guests may serve themselves.

Helping Hands

Help from the Seasoned Cook

Peeling shrimp for Todd's Shrimp and Grits and chopping fruit and making the emulsion of the Poppy Seed Dressing requires some skill.

Help from the Kids

Have an adult make the sausage ball mix and then turn it over to the kids to roll into jawbreaker-size balls. They can also crack the eggs and sift the flour for the Breakfast Bread Pudding. Greasing cake pans is a kid-friendly task as well.

This is also a great occasion for children to find flowers and greenery from the garden and be creative by filling simple vases with what they picked.

Egg Casserole

2 cups seasoned toasted croutons

1 cup shredded sharp Cheddar cheese

5 large eggs, slightly beaten

2 cups milk

½ teaspoon dry mustard

½ teaspoon salt

⅛ teaspoon onion powder

Dash of black pepper

Preheat the oven to 325°F. Grease a 9- by 13-inch baking dish.

Combine croutons and cheese and spread in the prepared dish.

In a large bowl, combine eggs, milk, dry mustard, salt, onion powder, and pepper. Mix well.

Pour over crouton mixture. Bake for 30 to 45 minutes, or until the top is puffy and golden brown.

Makes 8 servings

Kitchen Note

- You may sprinkle cooked crumbled bacon or sausage on top before baking.

Baked Canadian Bacon

2 pounds Canadian bacon, cut into ¼-inch-thick slices

¾ cup sugar

½ cup beer

½ teaspoon dry mustard

Preheat the oven to 350°F.

Place Canadian bacon on a jelly-roll pan.

In a medium bowl, combine sugar, beer, and mustard; stir to make a smooth paste. Spread paste over bacon.

Bake bacon for 12 to 15 minutes, or until it curls around the edges and paste caramelizes.

Makes 8 servings

Kitchen Note

- To make this simple recipe even easier, use presliced Canadian bacon.

Granny's Sausage Balls

10 ounces extra sharp white Cheddar

1 pound bulk sausage, crumbled

3½ cups Bisquick baking mix

Preheat the oven to 350°F. Line two large baking sheets with parchment paper.

Melt cheese in the top of a double boiler.

Add sausage and Bisquick and stir well.

Mix the dough by hand and roll into 1-inch balls. Place on the prepared sheets, baking in batches, if necessary.

Bake for 15 minutes, or until browned and cooked through.

Makes 3 to 4 dozen sausage balls

Kitchen Notes

- To improvise a double boiler, place a Pyrex or stainless-steel bowl over a saucepan of boiling water.
- If you have extra, these sausage balls freeze well.

Todd's Shrimp and Grits

4 cups cooked quick-cooking grits

2 cups shredded smoked Gouda cheese

2 cups + 4 tablespoons unsalted butter

3 teaspoons kosher salt

1 teaspoon white pepper

½ cup Worcestershire sauce

1 tablespoon garlic powder

Juice of 1 lemon

2 pounds medium shrimp, peeled and deveined (about 48 shrimp)

Chopped fresh parsley

In a large bowl, mix together grits, cheese, 4 tablespoons of the butter, 2 teaspoons of the salt, and the pepper and keep warm.

Melt remaining 2 cups butter in a large saucepan and blend in Worcestershire sauce, garlic powder, lemon juice, and remaining 1 teaspoon salt. Sauté for 1 minute.

Toss in shrimp and cook until cooked through, about 5 minutes. Remove from the heat.

Serve shrimp over grits, sprinkled with parsley.

Makes 8 servings

Fresh Fruit with Poppy Seed Dressing

Poppy Seed Dressing

1½ cups sugar

⅔ cup vinegar

2 teaspoons dry mustard

2 teaspoons salt

3 tablespoons onion juice

2 cups vegetable oil

3 tablespoons poppy seeds

Fresh Fruit Salad

2 green apples, unpeeled, cored, and chopped

2 red apples, unpeeled, cored, and chopped

Juice of 1 lemon

2 cups cubed cantaloupe or honeydew melon

1 cup golden raisins

½ cup red grapes, halved and seeded

To make dressing: In a blender, or with an electric mixer or food processor, mix sugar, vinegar, mustard, and salt. Add onion juice and blend in thoroughly.

Add oil slowly, beating constantly, and continue to beat until thick.

Add poppy seeds and beat for a few minutes. Store dressing in a cool place or in the refrigerator.

To make salad: Toss green and red apples with lemon juice in a serving bowl.

Stir in cantaloupe, raisins, and grapes.

Toss with enough dressing to coat fruit and serve.

Makes 8 servings

Kitchen Note

- Make onion juice by grating a large white onion on the fine side of a grater over a bowl to get 3 tablespoons.

Breakfast Bread Pudding
with Fresh Blueberry Syrup

Blueberry Syrup

2 cups blueberries

½ cup sugar

1 cinnamon stick

¼ teaspoon lemon juice

Bread Pudding

½ cup butter, softened

12 slices raisin bread

2 cups milk

6 large eggs

1 cup packed light brown sugar

1 teaspoon vanilla extract

Cream

To make syrup: Combine all syrup ingredients in a medium saucepan.

Bring to a boil and simmer for 10 minutes. Remove cinnamon stick.

Serve either warm or chilled.

To make bread pudding: Preheat the oven to 350°F. Use some of the butter to grease a 10- by 13-inch baking dish.

Spread remaining butter on bread slices and cut bread into ½-inch cubes. Place bread in the prepared dish.

Combine milk, eggs, brown sugar, and vanilla in a medium bowl; stir well.

Pour milk mixture over bread. Do not stir.

Bake for 35 to 40 minutes, or until firm. Let stand a few minutes before serving.

Serve hot with cream and blueberry syrup.

Makes 8 servings

Kitchen Notes

- This may be assembled and refrigerated overnight. Bring to room temperature before baking.
- Do not overcook the syrup as it will become jam instead of syrup.

Old-Fashioned Biscuits

2 cups all-purpose flour

1 tablespoon baking power

1 tablespoon sugar

1 teaspoon salt

1 cup heavy whipping cream, additional as needed

4 tablespoons unsalted butter, melted

Preheat the oven to 425°F. Lightly grease a baking sheet.

Combine flour, baking powder, sugar, and salt in a large bowl.

Gradually mix in enough cream to bind.

Turn dough out onto a floured surface and knead for about 30 seconds.

Pat into a ½-inch-thick round.

Cut out biscuits with a 2- or 2½-inch round cutter.

Dip each round into melted butter, coating top and sides and place biscuits, buttered tops up, on the prepared baking sheet.

Bake for 12 minutes, or until lightly browned.

Makes 10 to 12 biscuits

Kitchen Notes

For the best biscuits, follow these tips:

- When stirring the cream into the flour, only stir until the flour is just moist. Excessive stirring makes the biscuits tough.

- When cutting the biscuits, push the cutter into the dough and pull it straight out. Twisting the cutter will cause the biscuit not to rise as high.

- Leftover biscuits are good when sliced open and buttered for breakfast.

Breakfast Bundt Cake

2 cups sugar

1 cup unsalted butter

2 large eggs

1 cup sour cream

1 teaspoon vanilla extract

2 cups sifted all-purpose flour

1 teaspoon baking powder

¼ to ½ teaspoon salt

¾ cup chopped pecans

4 to 5 tablespoons brown sugar

2 teaspoons ground cinnamon

Confectioners' sugar (optional)

Preheat the oven to 350°F. Grease and flour a Bundt pan.

Place sugar and butter in the bowl of an electric mixer and beat until creamy.

Add eggs, one at a time, while continuing to beat.

Mix sour cream and vanilla together in a small bowl.

In a large bowl, sift flour, baking powder, and salt together.

Add flour mixture to butter alternately with sour cream, stirring between each addition.

Pour one-third to one-half of batter into the prepared pan.

Combine pecans, brown sugar, and cinnamon in a small bowl; sprinkle over cake batter.

Spoon remaining batter into cake pan.

Bake for 60 to 65 minutes, or until top is golden. Cake will rise, then fall slightly.

Cool for at least 10 minutes before removing from the pan.

Sift confectioners' sugar over top of warm cake, if desired.

Makes 10 to 12 servings

Kitchen Note

● Leftover cake is delicious sliced, buttered, and toasted.

CHAPTER 3

Fresh from the Blackberry Garden

for 6 guests

Blackberry Farm is a magical place. It's a fairy-tale setting where dreams come true for me and for the thousands of guests who find their way to the foothills of the Smoky Mountains to relax and recharge at the luxury resort.

Founded by my friend and mentor Kreis Beall, Blackberry Farm is now in the capable and creative hands of her son, Sam. I met Sam on my initial visit to Blackberry several years ago when my son, Martin, and I were guests. When I was invited to do my first "Camp Blackberry" cooking program for kids, his daughter Cameron was one of my first students. Cameron is known to legions of Blackberry guests as "Teensy," the nickname she earned as a small child when she showed up unexpectedly in the midst of guest activities. Teensy is to Blackberry as the fictional Eloise was to the famous Plaza Hotel in New York City, a spirited character roaming the property and lending her child's sense of wonder and inquisitiveness to all she encounters. She began cooking classes with me at age 4 and now, as an accomplished 10-year-old cook, is my valued assistant. I am pleased and proud that she shared her recipes with me for this book.

Sam has his mother's passion for creating the ultimate expression of hospitality and has taken her vision for this special property and expanded it. One of Sam's fervent dreams has been to create a working farm at Blackberry, including an organic vegetable garden. The garden has become a centerpiece for the classes I teach there each year. A Kitchen Full of Kids is a fun-filled 3-day cooking camp for children. The highlight takes place on the final day, when the kids prepare lunch for their parents. We begin the day prepping for our luncheon and making desserts.

Our desserts are just the thing for a summer picnic. Teensy's Chocolate Chip Treats are a favorite for kids and adults. And who doesn't love peanut butter and jelly? Our scrumptious PBJ Brownies add a new dimension to this beloved duo.

The recipe for Sylvie's Slushie Smoothie was a gift from Sylvie Palmer, a young cook who took my class. She sent the recipe with a note saying she makes this with her dad almost every morning. She said it's like starting the day with ice cream, except it's healthy! She thought it would be perfect for parents to sip before lunch. It's truly delicious, especially on a hot Tennessee summer day.

Creating sandwiches from the garden is the best part of our meal preparation. We spend time in the garden collecting our ingredients: picking tomatoes, lettuce, and dill; digging up potatoes, carrots, and sweet onions; choosing juicy strawberries, blueberries, and blackberries. With our baskets full of fruits and vegetables, we head to the kitchen, wash our garden bounty, and begin to cook.

The cooks range in age from 3 to 11. If you were to peek through the window as we prepare a parent lunch you might see Rose, who is 3, putting fresh fruit in ice cube trays for our Blackberry Lemonade, a variation on Front Porch Lemonade (see Kitchen Note, page 33). Five-year-old Sam is peeling carrots and 10-year-old Cameron is helping the other kids make treats she created. Parents, who wonder what we've been up to for 3 days, eagerly await their "special luncheon" and are always pleasantly surprised to see what accomplished chefs their little ones have become. It was especially rewarding to hear one parent say, "I would serve this luncheon for my friends."

Helping Hands

Help from the Seasoned Cook

Caramelizing onions for the onion dip and roasting vegetables for the wraps are jobs for a good cook. While these recipes aren't time consuming, they do require a little skill.

Help from the Kids

This menu was created by kids at Blackberry Farm, so children can make just about anything on this menu with adult assistance, particularly when working at the stove or using the oven. While an adult does the onions and roasts the vegetables, kids can skewer the fruit and make Teensy's Chocolate Chip Treats. My 3-year-old friend Rose loves to place blackberries in the ice cube trays to freeze for the Blackberry Lemonade.

Sylvie's Slushie Smoothie

This recipe makes 2 smoothies. Make it in three batches to serve 6.

1 cup 1% milk

2 cups frozen organic mixed berries

2 teaspoons vanilla-flavored protein powder

Pour milk into a blender and add berries and protein powder.

Mix on high speed for 1 minute, or until the ingredients are blended into a slushie smoothie.

Serve immediately in parfait glasses and eat with a spoon.

Makes 2 servings

Kitchen Note

- You could also make the smoothie with fresh berries and ice cubes. The key is that it should stay superthick and frosty.

- For a sweeter smoothie, add 1 tablespoon of sugar.

Caramelized Onion Dip

4 tablespoons unsalted butter

¼ cup vegetable oil

2 large Vidalia onions, thinly sliced

½ teaspoon Creole seasoning

1 teaspoon kosher salt

½ teaspoon black pepper

4 ounces cream cheese, at room temperature

½ cup mayonnaise

½ cup sour cream

Corn chips for dipping

Heat butter and oil in a large skillet over medium heat. Add onions, Creole seasoning, salt, and pepper and sauté for 10 to 12 minutes. Reduce the heat to medium-low and cook, stirring occasionally, until onions are browned and caramelized, 25 minutes longer. Remove from the heat and let cool slightly.

Beat cream cheese, mayonnaise, and sour cream in a medium bowl with a mixer until light and fluffy. Transfer to a serving bowl. Stir onions into cream cheese mixture, mixing well. Serve warm or at room temperature with corn chips.

Makes 6 servings

BLT Pita Pockets with Spicy Comeback Sauce

12 slices bacon

3 pita rounds

2 tablespoons Spicy Comeback Sauce (below)

6 lettuce leaves

2 medium tomatoes, each cut into 6 slices

Preheat the oven to 400°F.

Place bacon on a wire rack and set in a shallow pan. Bake 12 to 15 minutes, or until crisp. Let cool.

Cut pitas in half. Spread insides with sauce.

Place 1 lettuce leaf, 2 tomato slices, and 2 bacon slices in each pita pocket.

Makes 6 pockets

Spicy Comeback Sauce

1 medium onion, chopped

1 cup mayonnaise

½ cup chili sauce

½ cup ketchup

½ cup vegetable oil

3 cloves garlic, peeled

2 tablespoons fresh lemon juice

1 tablespoon paprika

1 tablespoon Worcestershire sauce

1½ teaspoons Creole seasoning

1 teaspoon dry mustard

Place all ingredients in a blender and pulse until blended.

Makes about 3 cups sauce

Kitchen Note

● The sauce can be stored in the refrigerator for up to 2 weeks! It's great as a salad dressing, too. In fact, I use it that way for the Field Greens and Romaine Salad (page 55).

BLT Pita Pockets with
Spicy Comeback Sauce (opposite),
Garden New Potato Salad (page 27),
and Blackberry Lemonade (page 33)

Roasted Vegetable Wraps

1 small eggplant, thinly sliced

1 red bell pepper, seeded and thinly sliced

1 yellow squash, thinly sliced

1 zucchini, thinly sliced

2 teaspoons extra-virgin olive oil

  Salt and black pepper

¼ cup sour cream

2 tablespoons mayonnaise

1 tablespoon chopped fresh basil

  Juice of ½ lemon

2 cloves garlic, minced

6 flour tortillas

Preheat the oven to 450°F.

Combine eggplant, bell pepper, yellow squash, and zucchini in a large roasting pan. Add oil and toss to coat. Season with salt and pepper. Roast vegetables for 20 minutes, or until tender.

Whisk together sour cream, mayonnaise, basil, lemon juice, and garlic in a small bowl. Spread some mayonnaise mixture on 1 tortilla and spoon ½ cup of vegetables down the center. Roll into a tight cylinder. Repeat with remaining tortillas.

Makes 6 servings

Kitchen Notes

- Use any vegetable of choice, especially those that are in season.
- You can also toss the roasted vegetables with angel hair pasta for a variation.

Garden New Potato Salad

8 or 9 new potatoes, quartered

¼ pound bacon, chopped

¼ cup finely chopped shallots

¼ cup red wine vinegar

2 tablespoons olive oil

Salt and black pepper

½ cup chopped fresh parsley

⅓ cup chopped red onion

Drop potatoes into a large heavy pot of cold, salted water. Bring to a boil and cook until tender but still firm, 8 to 10 minutes after water reaches a boil.

Fry bacon in a small skillet over medium-low heat until crisp. Remove bacon from the pan, drain on paper towels, and set aside.

In the bacon fat remaining in the skillet, sauté shallots until tender but not at all browned, about 5 minutes. Remove the pan from the heat and set aside.

Drain potatoes and transfer to a serving bowl.

Add vinegar, olive oil, and reserved shallots and bacon fat to potatoes while they are still hot. Season with salt and pepper and toss gently.

Add parsley and onion and toss again.

Cool to room temperature, and let sit at room temperature until ready to serve, up to 1 hour.

Before serving, toss salad, and check the seasonings. Add additional oil and vinegar if potato salad seems dry. Sprinkle the reserved crisp bacon on top.

Makes 6 servings

Teensy's Chocolate Chip Treats

This recipe was given to me by my friend Cameron Beall, also known as Teensy. She created these for family and friends and now makes them for some special guests at Blackberry Farm.

1 cup + 2 tablespoons all-purpose flour

½ teaspoon baking soda

10 tablespoons unsalted butter, softened

⅔ cup firmly packed light brown sugar

⅓ cup granulated sugar

1 large egg, preferably fresh from a farm

1½ teaspoons vanilla extract

¼ teaspoon salt

1 overflowing cup your favorite chocolate chips or chunks

Milk (optional)

Preheat the oven to 375°F. Line large baking sheets with parchment paper. Place a large drinking glass in the freezer.

In a medium bowl, whisk together flour and baking soda.

In a large stainless steel bowl, cream butter, brown sugar, and granulated sugar. Stir in egg, vanilla, and salt.

Incorporate flour mixture into butter mixture until smooth.

Stir in chocolate chips.

If time allows and you can wait, refrigerate dough for 15 to 20 minutes while you clean up.

Using a tablespoon, scoop dough 2 to 3 inches apart onto the prepared baking sheet.

Bake, rotating the sheets after 5 minutes, for 8 to 10 minutes, or until cookies are lightly browned and their centers are still slightly soft.

Repeat with remaining dough.

Let cookies cool on the baking sheets for 2 minutes, then transfer to wire racks to continue cooling.

Remove glass from freezer, pour milk, choose a cookie, and ENJOY!

Makes 2 to 2½ dozen treats

PBJ Brownies

1½ cups sugar

1 cup unsalted butter, at room temperature

2 cups creamy peanut butter

2 large eggs, at room temperature

1¼ teaspoons vanilla extract

3 cups all-purpose flour

1½ teaspoons salt

1 teaspoon baking powder

1 (18-ounce) jar strawberry jam

¾ cup salted peanuts

Preheat the oven to 350°F. Grease and flour a 9- by 13-inch baking pan.

Place sugar and butter in the bowl of an electric mixer and beat on medium speed until well blended.

Add peanut butter, eggs, and vanilla and mix until well combined.

In a separate large bowl, sift together flour, salt, and baking powder.

Slowly add flour mixture to peanut butter mixture. Mix just until combined. Do not overmix.

Press two-thirds of dough evenly in the prepared pan. Spread jam evenly over dough. Drop small globs of the remaining dough evenly over jam.

Place peanuts in a zip-top bag. Crush by rolling a rolling pin over peanuts. Sprinkle crushed peanuts over top of brownies.

Bake brownies for 40 minutes, or until golden brown.

Cool in the pan before cutting.

Makes 2 to 3 dozen brownies, depending on the size you cut them

CHAPTER 4

Neighborhood Gathering Picnic

for 8 guests

My family will picnic just about anywhere and on a moment's notice. At our house, picnics traditionally begin with patchwork quilts scattered around the yard. A quilt on the ground creates a relaxed and inviting atmosphere that attracts everyone from babies to grandparents. A big yard is not a requirement, as creativity is the only ingredient necessary for a successful picnic. One can be staged on a patio, a porch, or by bringing the feel of the outdoors inside the house.

A neighborhood picnic is the perfect vehicle for children and adults to enjoy each other in a relaxed setting. The key ingredient for any successful picnic is to keep things simple. This is a time to forget about using good dishes, and instead offer functional but attractive paper plates and accessories.

When planning picnic food, keep in mind that everything should be easy to eat and appealing to all ages. Sandwiches are versatile for feeding groups, but make sure to offer special salads and sides for the adults. In preparing a sandwich tray, I find it's always a good idea to add a few peanut butter and jelly sandwiches to cover emergency situations with small children or picky eaters.

Cold zucchini soup in colorful paper cups is a good way to start a picnic, and lemonade for the children is a must. Lemonade becomes a special treat if children are allowed to help by squeezing the lemons and stirring the lemonade. For the more adventurous, setting up a lemonade stand is a worthy picnic enterprise. I come from a long line of lemonade entrepreneurs, starting with my mom and her sister Mary, who ran a popular lemonade business from a card table in front of their home on Main Street in Hattiesburg, Mississippi. The recipe for Front Porch Lemonade was perfected by my friend and student Clara Frances Cannon, a veteran of numerous lemonade stands, who will no doubt achieve fame and fortune for her expert sales ability.

One of my most unforgettable picnics was a beautiful backyard bridesmaids' luncheon at my mom's home. The bride-to-be and her bridesmaids were seated on quilts scattered around the yard and each was handed a yellow basket lined with a colorful cloth and packed with a sandwich, pasta salad, fruit cup, and a small bottle of champagne and a plastic flute. A trio of stuffed eggs was passed on a flat woven basket decorated with fresh herbs and flowers. The eggs featured a traditional stuffing along with two newer versions, one with fresh basil and the other with sun-dried tomatoes. The lively picnic was a memorable beginning to the wedding festivities.

Like stuffed eggs, pimento cheese is usually found somewhere in a Southern picnic basket. Spicy and creamy, it's delicious on sandwiches, stuffed in celery, or as a dip with crackers or corn chips. This version comes from the kitchen of my sister-in-law Susie Hand Puckett, whose well-traveled picnic basket is filled with delicious high-energy foods as she moves from soccer fields to baseball diamonds with her four active boys.

Fried chicken is a perfect picnic food and I'm sharing the perfect recipe. On a recent trip to Chicago, I stopped in at my friend Art Smith's restaurant, Table Fifty-Two. Knowing that all Southerners consider themselves experts on matters of chicken, he encouraged me to taste his buttermilk fried chicken. I pronounced it absolutely heavenly and was thrilled that Art gave me his recipe.

Cornbread Salad is not only tasty but also makes an impressive picnic presentation when served in an acrylic salad bowl. Dressed up in a footed glass trifle bowl, it's also an indoor favorite for brunch, lunch, or a special celebration. Slices of tomatoes drizzled with extra virgin olive oil and sprinkled with a chiffonade of fresh basil are an optional addition to this menu.

A well-planned picnic calls for easy cleanup and, because everyone loves picnic foods, leftovers are usually minimal. Guests leave happy and the host feels the satisfaction that comes from creating a small interval of camaraderie and magic in our everyday lives.

Helping Hands

Help from the Seasoned Cook

After it's been brined, then marinated (this takes 2 days), Art's Buttermilk Fried Chicken Tenders can be made several hours in advance of your gathering and be served at room temperature. Have a person who's experienced with deep-fat frying do the work here.

Help from the Kids

Peeling eggs and mashing yolks is an easy and helpful task. Once the fillings are prepared, kids can also stuff the eggs. Front Porch Lemonade is a sure success when made and served by any child. After all, they are the pros at running a lemonade stand.

Front Porch Lemonade

1¼ cups sugar

½ cup boiling water

1½ cups fresh lemon juice

4½ cups cold water

Lemon slices for garnish (optional)

Combine sugar and boiling water in a large heatproof bowl or pitcher, stirring until sugar dissolves.

Add lemon juice and cold water and mix well. Chill.

Serve over ice, garnished with lemon slices, if desired.

Makes 8 servings

Blackberry Lemonade

This is a favorite at Blackberry Farm (see menu, page 20). Adding special blackberry ice cubes to Front Porch Lemonade turns it into "Blackberry Lemonade." To make the cubes, place one or two blackberries in each compartment of an ice cube tray. Fill the compartments with water and freeze. You can also use any other fruit of your choice.

Cold Zucchini Soup

5 medium zucchini, thinly sliced

1 large yellow onion, sliced

1 large baking potato, peeled and thinly sliced

4 teaspoons unsalted butter

3 cups chicken broth

1 pint half-and-half

2 teaspoons salt

1 teaspoon sugar

1 teaspoon soy sauce

½ teaspoon black pepper

Combine zucchini, onion, potato, and butter in a heavy pot. Cover and cook slowly, stirring occasionally, until vegetables are very tender, about 15 minutes.

In batches, process vegetables in a food processor until smooth. Transfer to a large bowl. Stir in broth, half-and-half, salt, sugar, soy sauce, and pepper. Cover and chill.

Serve cold.

Makes 8 servings

Art's Buttermilk Fried Chicken Tenders

Keep in mind that you'll need to start this recipe 2 days ahead of serving in order to have time to brine it and marinate it to perfection.

½ gallon water

¼ cup kosher salt

8 boneless skinless chicken breasts, cut into strips

1 quart buttermilk

1 tablespoon hot sauce

2 cups self-rising flour

2 teaspoons garlic powder

1 teaspoon Old Bay seasoning

1 teaspoon cayenne pepper

1 teaspoon black pepper

Grape seed oil for frying

Combine water and salt in a large bowl and stir for a few minutes to make a brine solution.

Submerge chicken pieces in the brine. Cover and refrigerate overnight.

Remove chicken from brine; discard brine. Rinse chicken and return to the bowl.

Combine buttermilk and hot sauce in a medium bowl. Pour over chicken, cover, and marinate overnight in the refrigerator.

Sift flour, garlic powder, Old Bay, cayenne, and black pepper into a shallow dish to evenly distribute the spices.

Remove chicken from buttermilk and shake off as much liquid as possible. Dredge a couple of pieces of chicken in flour mixture, then dip in buttermilk. Shake off the excess and dredge again in the flour.

Repeat with the remaining chicken pieces. Chicken can be set on a tray for a short period, but fry it quickly so that coating does not fall off.

In a cast-iron skillet, heat 1 inch of oil to 375°F over high heat. Use a thermometer to make sure oil is the correct temperature.

Using tongs, carefully lower chicken into hot oil, a few pieces at a time. Do not crowd the skillet. Cook chicken until browned on one side, 6 to 7 minutes. Turn over and cook on the other side until cooked through.

Carefully remove chicken and drain on paper towels.

Repeat with remaining chicken. Serve hot or at room temperature.

Makes 8 servings

Art's Buttermilk Fried Chicken Tenders (opposite)
with Salad of Fresh Greens and Strawberries with Strawberry Vinaigrette (page 36).

Salad of Fresh Greens and Strawberries with Strawberry Vinaigrette

Strawberry Vinaigrette

- 1 cup strawberries, hulled and halved
- ¼ cup olive oil
- 2 tablespoons brown sugar
- 2 tablespoons raspberry vinegar
- ½ teaspoon fresh lemon juice
- ¼ teaspoon sesame oil

  Kosher salt and black pepper

Salad

- 4 cups mixed greens
- 1½ cups strawberries, hulled and halved
- 1 medium English cucumber, sliced
- ½ red onion, sliced
- ¼ cup toasted pistachios, chopped

To make vinaigrette: Process strawberries, olive oil, brown sugar, vinegar, lemon juice, and sesame oil in a food processor or blender until smooth. Season with salt and pepper.

To make salad: Combine greens, strawberries, cucumber, and onion in a salad bowl.

Just before serving, toss dressing with salad and sprinkle with pistachios.

Makes 8 servings

Kitchen Note

- To toast pistachios: Preheat the oven to 350°F. Spread the pistachios on a baking sheet and toast for 8 minutes, or until golden brown.

Susie's Pimento Cheese Sandwiches

2 cups finely shredded sharp Cheddar cheese

2 cups finely shredded Monterey Jack and Colby cheese blend or 1 cup each

1 cup good-quality mayonnaise

4 green onions, finely chopped

½ teaspoon Greek seasoning, such as Cavendar's

Salt and black pepper

¾ cup toasted pecans, chopped

1 (4-ounce) jar diced pimentos, drained

1 loaf sliced farmhouse white bread, crusts removed

Butter lettuce, washed, separated, and dried

Mix together cheeses in a large bowl.

In a separate bowl, combine mayonnaise, green onions, Greek seasoning, salt, and pepper.

Stir mayonnaise mixture into cheeses. Add pecans and pimentos. Season with additional salt and pepper if desired.

Spread 2 to 3 tablespoons pimento cheese on 1 slice of bread. Top with a lettuce leaf and second slice of bread.

Repeat to make remaining sandwiches.

Cut into triangles or halves.

Makes 8 to 10 servings

Kitchen Notes

- To make ahead, put completed sandwiches in a plastic container, placing a dampened paper towel between layers and on top. Cover tightly. These will keep overnight.
- To toast the pecans, spread on a baking sheet and bake in 250°F oven for 5 to 7 minutes.

Cornbread Salad

This recipe makes enough to enjoy the leftovers another day, unless of course your guests devour it all. Keep leftovers in the refrigerator for up to a day.

1 cup mayonnaise

1 cup sour cream

1 (0.4-ounce) package Hidden Valley ranch buttermilk dressing mix

3 large tomatoes, chopped

½ cup chopped green bell pepper

½ cup chopped green onions

Sliced jalapeño chiles to taste

1 (8.5-ounce) box Jiffy corn muffin mix, prepared according to package instructions, cooled, and crumbled

2 (16-ounce) cans black beans, drained

2 cups shredded Cheddar cheese

2 (17-ounce) cans whole corn kernels, drained and rinsed

10 slices bacon, cooked and crumbled

1 cup salsa

For the dressing, combine mayonnaise, sour cream, and dressing mix in a medium bowl.

Combine tomatoes, bell pepper, green onions, and jalapeño chiles in another medium bowl.

In a large glass serving bowl, begin layering: Place half of the cornbread crumbs on the bottom of the bowl. Top with layers of half of the black beans, tomato mixture, cheese, corn, bacon, and dressing.

Repeat layers.

Top with salsa. Let sit at room temperature for at least 4 hours before serving.

Makes 10 to 12 servings

Kitchen Notes

- The dressing, tomato mixture, and cornbread may be prepared a day ahead and refrigerated; do not mix to prevent salad from getting soggy. To save a little bit of time, you can use store-bought cornbread.

- The bacon can also be cooked ahead and crumbled.

- You may use pinto beans instead of black beans.

An Assortment of Stuffed Eggs

2 dozen large eggs (preferably several days old)

½ cup mayonnaise (homemade is best)

6 to 8 drops fresh lemon juice

2 or 3 dashes Tabasco sauce

Dash Worcestershire sauce

Salt and black pepper

Paprika

Basic Eggs

1 tablespoon sweet pickle relish, drained

1½ teaspoons Durkee Famous Sauce

Chopped fresh chives for garnish

Pesto Eggs

½ cup pine nuts, toasted (see page 170)

2 tablespoons prepared basil pesto

Chiffonade of fresh basil, for garnish (see Kitchen Notes page 76)

Sun-Dried Tomato Eggs

2 tablespoons sun-dried tomato pesto

¼ cup sun-dried tomatoes packed in oil, blotted dry, and finely chopped

Additional sun-dried tomatoes, blotted and cut into strips, for garnish

Cover eggs with cold water in a large pot and bring to a rapid boil. Cover and cook for 15 minutes.

Run cold water over eggs to cool. Peel and cut each egg in half.

Place egg yolks in a bowl and mash. Add mayonnaise, lemon juice, Tabasco, Worcestershire, salt, and pepper to yolks and mash to desired consistency.

Divide yolk mixture among 3 bowls.

To make basic eggs: Mix relish and Durkee sauce into one bowl of yolk mixture.

Fill 16 egg white halves with the mixture. Garnish with chopped chives.

To make pesto eggs: Mix all but 2 tablespoons pine nuts and the basil pesto into second bowl of yolk mixture.

Fill 16 halved egg whites with mixture. Garnish with remaining 2 tablespoons pine nuts and basil.

To make sun-dried tomato eggs: Mix tomato pesto and chopped sun-dried tomatoes into remaining bowl of yolk mixture.

Fill 16 halved egg whites with the mixture. Garnish with strips of sun-dried tomatoes.

Makes 48 stuffed eggs

Lemon Squares

Crust

3 cups all-purpose flour

1½ cups unsalted butter, at room temperature

¾ cup confectioners' sugar, plus more for sprinkling

Filling

3 cups granulated sugar

6 tablespoons all-purpose flour

6 large eggs

6 tablespoons lemon juice

3 tablespoons grated lemon zest

To make crust: Preheat the oven to 350°F.

Cream together all crust ingredients in a large bowl.

Press crust mixture into a 12- by 16-inch jelly-roll pan.

Bake for 15 minutes, or until set.

Meanwhile, to make filling: Mix together all filling ingredients in another large bowl. Pour filling over crust.

Bake for 15 minutes longer, or until set.

Cool and cut into squares. Sprinkle with confectioners' sugar.

Makes 2 to 3 dozen squares

Kitchen Notes

- To easily sprinkle confectioners' sugar, put several tablespoons in a small strainer and gently shake over the lemon squares.

- The lemon squares can be made a day ahead and stored in an airtight container.

- Citrus zest is only the colored portion of the skin of the fruit. Use a citrus zester or microplane zester for easy "zesting" and to avoid getting any of the white pith. Press the fruit firmly down on the zester as you scrape over a bowl.

The Very Best Blondies

¾ cup unsalted butter

1 (16-ounce) box brown sugar

2 cups all-purpose flour

1 teaspoon baking powder

½ teaspoon baking soda

2 large eggs, well beaten

2 teaspoons vanilla extract

1 cup pecans

1 cup semisweet chocolate chips

Preheat the oven to 350°F. Grease a 10- by 13-inch Pyrex baking dish.

Melt butter and pour over brown sugar in a large bowl. Mix well. Let cool.

Combine flour, baking powder, and baking soda.

Add flour mixture and eggs alternately to butter mixture, beginning and ending with flour. Add vanilla and mix well.

Fold in pecans.

Spread batter in the prepared baking dish. Sprinkle chocolate chips on top. Bake for 20 minutes, or until golden brown.

Makes 2 dozen blondies

Kitchen Note

● The blondies can be made a day ahead and stored in an airtight container.

CHAPTER 5

Soup Around the Fireplace

for 8 guests

Last winter I signed up for a book study during the Lenten season at my Episcopal church. Mine was the host home and others in the group led the discussion each week. When asked if I would agree to be the host for 5 weeks, I eagerly said yes, but only if I could serve soup and salad before the meeting began. From my experience as a single mother who worked outside the home, I recalled too vividly the frantic rush to evening meetings on an empty stomach. I knew that food and fellowship at the table would set a more relaxed tone for the book study ahead.

I called my dear friend Marsha, whose business is called Simply Organized, and told her what I'd agreed to do. After telling me I was crazy, we put her formidable organizational skills to the test. Marsha helped me get my small house in order so that each week it would be easy to set a table for 8. We organized the china closet, making the serving pieces easy to access. We pulled out pretty dishes and silver that were carefully tucked away for special occasions. We dug out my "nice" tablecloths and napkins, ironed them, and placed them in a convenient drawer. The old saying "out of sight, out of mind" perfectly described my situation. Tucked away in closets and cabinets, I discovered hidden treasures and beloved accessories. With her help, I made entertaining in my home easy—or as Marsha would say "simple." Now that everything is in sight, in order, and easy to access, I entertain at the drop of a hat.

Each week for the study group I enjoyed creating and cooking different menus from the assortment of soups, breads, and desserts you'll find in this chapter. The fun is to mix, match, and create your own menu according to the occasion. This chapter offers you a wide variety of recipes from which to pick and choose, creating just the right combination for you and your guests. Croutons, biscuits, and toasts are the "something extra" that transform any soup or salad into something special. They're surprisingly easy to make and well worth the effort! The desserts are all designed to be picked up. My mother, who serves as my expert advisor on entertaining, taught me to always make "pick-up" desserts when trying to keep a meal simple. No silverware or plates are required; a pretty cocktail napkin is all you need.

Hosting the book study turned out to be one of life's unexpected blessings and one of the most fun things I've done for myself. We started out as strangers and acquaintances, but through our fellowship of shared meals and ideas we became good friends. In fact, when the Lenten season was past, we decided to keep this spirited group together and continue our suppers and study.

Helping Hands

Help from the Seasoned Cook

The smoked tomatoes and onions for the tomato soup require grilling skills. A patient cook is necessary to prep all the ingredients for the Chicken Gumbo, and there are several steps involved in making it. Start the day before and you'll be ahead of schedule. Kahlúa Brownies are a favorite for a seasoned baker.

Help from the Kids

Kids will be surprised at how much they like Orzo and Edamame Soup. They can cut the tofu and let an adult toss everything in the pot. Buttering pitas for the Pita Toasts and spreading goat cheese on the croutons are other kid-friendly tasks.

Artichoke and Mushroom Soup

6 tablespoons unsalted butter

8 ounces fresh mushrooms, sliced

1 bunch green onions, chopped

¼ cup all-purpose flour

2 cups chicken broth

2 cups half-and-half

½ cup dry white wine

1 (14-ounce) can artichoke hearts, drained and chopped

½ teaspoon salt

¼ teaspoon cayenne pepper

Melt butter in a large saucepan over medium heat. Add mushrooms and green onions and sauté until tender.

Stir in flour until well blended. Remove the pan from the heat and let mushroom mixture cool slightly.

Return the pan to medium heat and gradually stir in broth, half-and-half, and wine. Cook over medium heat, stirring often, until just thickened and hot.

Stir in artichoke hearts, salt, and cayenne. Cook until heated through. Do not overcook or the soup will become too thick.

Makes 8 servings

Kitchen Notes

- You can add a variety of different mushrooms. In a hurry? Presliced fresh mushrooms are a real time-saver.

- For variation, garnish with crumbled blue cheese or goat cheese.

Crab and Corn Bisque

Savory Whipped Cream

1 cup heavy cream

1 teaspoon Creole seasoning

Dash Tabasco sauce

Dash garlic salt

Bisque

8 ounces bacon

1 medium white onion, chopped

4 tablespoons unsalted butter

1 (15-ounce) can cream-style corn or
1 (20-ounce) package frozen cream-style
corn

3 (11-ounce) cans vacuum-packed shoepeg
corn (small kerneled white corn)

2 (14-ounce) cans chicken broth

¼ teaspoon cayenne pepper

¼ teaspoon garlic powder

Creole seasoning, to taste

Salt and black pepper

2 pounds lump crabmeat, picked through
to remove any pieces of shell

4 cups half-and-half

To make whipped cream: Whip cream to soft peaks in a large bowl using a hand mixer.

Fold in Creole seasoning, Tabasco, and garlic salt.

Cover and refrigerate until ready to serve.

To make bisque: Fry bacon in a Dutch oven over medium heat. Reserving fat in the pan, transfer bacon to paper towels to drain. When cooled, crumble bacon and set aside for garnish.

Add onion and butter to bacon fat and cook until onion is translucent.

Add both types of corn and chicken broth and bring to a boil. Cook over medium heat, stirring constantly, for 5 minutes. Add cayenne, garlic powder, Creole seasoning, salt, and pepper. Reduce heat and simmer for 15 minutes longer, stirring often.

Add crabmeat and half-and-half, reduce heat to low, and heat through.

Serve in individual bowls, garnished with savory whipped cream and crumbled bacon.

Makes 8 servings

Kitchen Note

● Gently stir the crabmeat—you do not want to break the lumps.

Crab and Corn Bisque (opposite)
with Pita Toasts (page 55).

Baked Onion Soup

5 tablespoons unsalted butter

7 cups thinly sliced yellow onions (about 6 onions)

3 tablespoons all-purpose flour

8 cups beef broth

¾ cup dry white wine

1 teaspoon salt

¾ teaspoon black pepper

3 tablespoons brandy

8 slices French bread, toasted

8 slices Gruyère cheese

1¼ cups freshly grated Parmesan cheese

Preheat the oven to 375°F.

Melt butter in a large saucepan. Add onions and sauté over medium heat until lightly browned, about 15 minutes.

Add flour and stir to blend well.

Stir in broth, wine, salt, and pepper. Bring to a boil. Reduce the heat and simmer for 10 minutes. Stir in brandy during last couple minutes of cooking.

Place a slice of bread in the bottom of 8 individual ovenproof soup bowls. Ladle soup over bread, top with Gruyère, and sprinkle with Parmesan.

Bake for about 5 minutes, or until cheese melts. Serve immediately.

Makes 8 servings

Kitchen Note

● Chicken broth can be substituted for beef broth, if desired.

Smoked Tomato Soup with Basil Cream

Tomato Soup

Smoking chips (mesquite, hickory, or pecan) for flavoring

4 pounds tomatoes

1 pound yellow onions

2 tablespoons olive oil

4 cloves garlic, minced

2 tablespoons tomato paste

1 quart chicken stock

Salt and black pepper

Basil Cream

¼ cup sour cream

2 tablespoons fresh basil

Juice of ½ lemon

Salt and black pepper

To make soup: Prepare a charcoal grill. When the coals are starting to coat with ash, put on a handful of smoking chips.

Cut half of the tomatoes in half. Cut half of the onions into thick rounds.

Place halved tomatoes and onion slices on the grill. Cover and smoke for 10 minutes. Remove from grill and reserve.

Coarsely chop remaining tomatoes and onions.

In a stockpot, heat olive oil over medium heat and add chopped onions and garlic. Sauté until translucent, about 7 minutes. Stirring constantly, add tomato paste and heat through.

Add chopped tomatoes and reserved grilled vegetables. Cover with stock and bring to a boil. Reduce heat and simmer until vegetables are very soft, 20 to 25 minutes.

Process soup in a blender or food processor, in batches if necessary, until smooth. Pass through a coarse strainer. Season with salt and pepper and reheat until hot.

Meanwhile, make basil cream: Process sour cream, basil, and lemon juice in a blender or mini food processor until smooth. Add salt and pepper to taste.

Serve soup hot, topped with basil cream.

Makes 8 servings

Kitchen Notes

- Using hardwood chips like mesquite, hickory, or pecan adds a distinctive flavor to the grilled vegetables. If you have a gas grill, follow the instructions that come with the wood chips. You can also use a stovetop smoker to grill the tomatoes and onions.

- As a variation, roast the tomatoes and onions in a 250°F oven for 1 hour.

Chicken and Sausage Gumbo

Roux

⅔ cup all-purpose flour

⅔ cup vegetable oil

Gumbo

6 boneless, skinless chicken thighs

6 tablespoons all-purpose flour

5 tablespoons oil

1½ pounds andouille sausage, cut into ½-inch-thick slices

2 large onions, chopped

1 bell pepper, seeded and chopped

1 cup chopped celery

2½ quarts chicken stock

3 cloves garlic, minced

½ teaspoon dried basil

½ teaspoon dried thyme

¼ teaspoon cayenne pepper, or to taste

3 bay leaves

⅛ teaspoon allspice

⅛ teaspoon ground cloves

Salt and black pepper

Cooked rice for serving

½ cup chopped green onions, for garnish

To make roux in the microwave: Mix together flour and oil in a microwavable bowl. Microwave on high for 6 minutes. Remove and stir. It should be slightly brown at this point.

To make a darker roux, microwave for 1 minute longer and stir. Continue to microwave and stir at 1-minute intervals until you reach the desired color. Set aside.

To make gumbo: Dust chicken with flour.

Heat oil in a Dutch oven. Add chicken and cook, turning, until browned. Leaving oil in the pan, transfer chicken to paper towels to drain.

Cook sausage in oil remaining in the pan until browned, about 10 minutes. Drain on paper towels and reserve with chicken. Discard all but 2 tablespoons of the oil. Add roux, onions, bell pepper, and celery to the pan. Sauté until vegetables are softened. Add stock, garlic, basil, thyme, cayenne, bay leaves, allspice, and cloves. Add reserved chicken and sausage. Cook slowly for about 2 hours, or until chicken is tender and begins to fall apart.

Discard bay leaves. Season gumbo with salt and pepper. Serve over warm rice, garnished with green onions.

Makes 8 servings

Kitchen Note

● Making a roux in the microwave saves on stirring effort at the stovetop. You can, of course, make the roux on the stove, stirring constantly, if you don't have a microwave oven.

Cheddar Cheese Soup with Apples and Smoked Bacon

8 thick slices smoked bacon, put in 2 stacks of 4 and cut into ¼-inch pieces

1 onion, coarsely chopped

4 green apples

4 red apples

1 clove garlic, minced

5 cups chicken broth

1 pound sharp Cheddar cheese, grated

Worcestershire sauce, to taste

Tabasco sauce, to taste

Lemon juice, to taste

Salt

In a 2-quart saucepan, cook bacon over medium-high heat until almost crisp. Transfer one-fourth of bacon to paper towels to drain and reserve for garnish. Leave rest of bacon in the pan.

Pour off half the bacon fat. Return the pan to medium heat. Add onion and sauté until lightly caramelized, about 7 minutes.

While onion is cooking, core and coarsely chop 3 green apples and 3 red apples (sprinkle with a little lemon juice to keep from discoloring).

Add garlic to pan and sauté for 1 minute.

Add chopped apples and sauté for 5 minutes.

Add chicken broth and simmer for 5 minutes.

Reserve ¼ cup of the cheese for garnish. Whisk remaining cheese into soup and cook over medium heat until soup is slightly thickened and cheese is melted.

Process soup in blender or food processor until smooth. Strain through a medium strainer and return to pan.

Adjust seasonings to your taste with drops of Worcestershire sauce, Tabasco sauce, lemon juice, and a sprinkling of salt. Reheat.

Just before serving, core and cut remaining red apple and green apple into ¼-inch dice. Garnish soup with diced apples and the reserved bacon and grated cheese.

Makes 8 servings

Kitchen Note

- Don't dice the apples for garnish too soon or they will turn brown. Once diced, tossing with a little lemon juice will prevent discoloration.

Orzo and Edamame Soup

"We came up with this soup with our mom. We started with just chicken broth and pasta… but then we added edamame, our favorite vegetable with green power! When we found out we liked tofu, we threw that in the pot, too. We like the fact that it all cooks in one pot and that we can cut the tofu ourselves and the rest is already small enough without being chopped up. Although we measured the ingredients for this recipe, a little more or less works just as well."

–Sylvie and William Palmer, students at Kitchen Full of Kids, Blackberry Farm

4 (14-ounce) cans low-sodium chicken broth

1⅓ cups orzo

2 cups frozen shelled edamame

10 ounces firm tofu (about two-thirds of 15.5-ounce container), cut into 1-inch cubes

1 teaspoon dark soy sauce

Bring broth to a boil in a large saucepan over moderately low heat. Add orzo and cook according to package directions until almost al dente, about 15 minutes. Reduce heat to low and add edamame. Simmer for 5 minutes. Stir in tofu and soy sauce and serve immediately.

Makes 8 servings

Baby Greens with Radicchio, Pears, and Blue Cheese

¼ cup olive oil

2 tablespoons minced shallots

2 tablespoons sherry vinegar

1 tablespoon + 1 teaspoon honey

2 teaspoons lemon juice

Salt and black pepper

2 cups mixed baby greens

2 cups finely sliced radicchio

2 small ripe pears, quartered, cored, and thinly sliced

½ cup crumbled blue cheese

Whisk oil, shallots, vinegar, honey, and lemon juice in a large serving bowl. Season dressing with salt and pepper. Add baby greens, radicchio, and pears to dressing and toss gently to coat. Serve salad on individual plates, sprinkled with blue cheese.

Makes 8 servings

Field Greens and Romaine with Spicy Comeback Dressing

The Spicy Comeback Sauce on page 24 makes a great dressing for this salad.

2 heads green leaf lettuce, washed and torn

1 head romaine lettuce, washed and torn

2 cups grape tomatoes

1 red bell pepper, chopped

1 orange bell pepper, chopped

Garlic salt

Spicy Comeback Sauce (page 24)

Combine leaf lettuce, romaine, tomatoes, and peppers in a large serving bowl.

Season with plenty of garlic salt to taste.

Serve with Spicy Comeback Sauce as the dressing.

Makes 8 servings

Pita Toasts

6 tablespoons unsalted butter, at room temperature

Juice of ½ lemon

1 tablespoon minced flat-leaf parsley

1 small clove garlic, minced

Salt and black pepper

5 pocket pita rounds

Process butter, lemon juice, parsley, garlic, salt, and pepper in a mini food processor until creamy. Transfer to a small bowl and let stand at least 1 hour.

Preheat the oven to 450°F.

Split pita rounds into halves. Spread halves with butter mixture. Cut each half into 6 or 8 triangles with kitchen shears.

Bake triangles on baking sheets for 5 minutes, or until lightly browned and crisp.

Makes 5 to 6 dozen toasts

Goat Cheese Croutons

1 long, thin French baguette

Olive oil

8 ounces goat cheese, softened

Preheat the oven to 350°F.

Cut bread into 24 (¼- to ½-inch-thick) rounds.

Place rounds on a baking sheet and brush with olive oil. Bake for 4 to 5 minutes, or until pale golden.

Spread some goat cheese on each round.

Return the croutons to the oven for 4 to 5 minutes, or until the tops are lightly browned.

Makes 2 dozen croutons

Kitchen Note

- Add fresh herbs of your choice to the softened goat cheese before spreading on the toasts.

Cheese Biscuits

2 cups Bisquick baking mix

1⅓ cups milk

1½ cups shredded sharp Cheddar cheese

2 large eggs

¼ cup sugar

⅛ to ¼ teaspoon cayenne pepper

Preheat the oven to 400°F. Grease 2 (12-cup) mini muffin tins.

Mix all ingredients together in a large bowl and stir vigorously for 1 minute.

Fill muffin cups two-thirds full with batter. Bake for 10 to 12 minutes, or until lightly golden.

Makes 24 biscuits

Kitchen Notes

- The biscuits will fall in the middle.

- Leftovers are delicious when toasted. Split the biscuits, butter both sides, and toast in a 350°F oven for about 3 minutes, or until butter is melted.

Coconut Squares

Crust

1½ cups unsalted butter

1½ cups firmly packed brown sugar

1¼ teaspoons salt

3 cups all-purpose flour

Topping

3 cups firmly packed brown sugar

6 large eggs

1 tablespoon vanilla extract

4½ cups sweetened flaked coconut

3 cups chopped pecans

6 tablespoons all-purpose flour

1½ teaspoons baking powder

To make crust: Preheat the oven to 350°F. Grease and flour a 10- by 16-inch jelly-roll pan.

Cream butter, brown sugar, and salt in a large bowl. Add flour and blend well.

Press dough into prepared pan.

Bake for 15 minutes, or until lightly browned.

Meanwhile, to make topping: Beat brown sugar, eggs, and vanilla in a medium bowl until light.

Add coconut, pecans, flour, and baking powder. Blend well.

Spread topping over partially baked crust.

Bake for 25 minutes longer, or until topping is firm.

Let cool and cut into squares.

Makes 2 to 3 dozen squares

Kahlúa Brownies

Crust

⅓ cup firmly packed light brown sugar

5 tablespoons unsalted butter, at room temperature

⅔ cup all-purpose flour, sifted

½ cup finely chopped pecans

Filling

2 ounces unsweetened chocolate

¼ cup shortening

4 tablespoons unsalted butter

½ cup firmly packed light brown sugar

½ cup granulated sugar

2 large eggs

1½ teaspoons vanilla extract

¼ cup Kahlúa

½ cup all-purpose flour, sifted

¼ teaspoon salt

½ cup chopped pecans

Creamy Frosting

2 cups sifted confectioners' sugar

6 tablespoons unsalted butter, softened

1½ tablespoons heavy whipping cream

1 tablespoon Kahlúa

Chocolate Glaze

2 ounces semisweet chocolate

1 ounce unsweetened chocolate

2 tablespoons shortening

Preheat the oven to 350°F. Grease and flour a 9-inch square baking pan.

To make crust: Cream sugar and butter in a large bowl until light and fluffy. Slowly add flour and continue to mix until well blended. Fold in pecans until completely combined.

Press dough into bottom of the prepared pan and set aside.

To make filling: Combine chocolate, shortening, and butter in a small saucepan over low heat. Stir until chocolate is melted and mixture is smooth. Let cool.

Combine brown sugar, granulated sugar, eggs, and vanilla in a large bowl. Mix until blended. Stir egg mixture into cooled chocolate mixture. Stir in Kahlúa. Slowly add flour and salt, mixing until batter is well blended. Fold in pecans.

Spread filling on prepared crust. Bake for 25 minutes, or until firm. Be careful not to overbake. Let cool in the pan.

To make frosting: Stir together confectioners' sugar, butter, cream, and Kahlúa in a medium bowl until smooth and creamy.

Spread over cooled filling and refrigerate for 30 minutes.

To make glaze: In a small saucepan, melt semisweet and unsweetened chocolates and shortening over low heat, stirring constantly. Let cool.

Drizzle glaze over frosting.

Makes 1½ dozen brownies

CHAPTER 6

Fall Is in the Air

for 8 guests

Autumn comes late to my Mississippi home. The hot, sticky temperatures finally dissolve into cool, crisp nights and we celebrate the change of seasons with spirited gatherings ranging from Halloween carnivals and tailgating picnics to festive fall dinner parties.

As the leaves change, so do our taste buds. We long for heavier, heartier dishes with the flavors of autumn fruits and vegetables. The local farmers' market dresses in fall colors with pumpkins of all shapes and sizes, sugarcane stalks, a dizzying array of squash, sacks of pecans waiting to be shelled, and an abundance of my favorite fall and winter vegetable, Brussels sprouts. Apples are stacked in baskets, inviting us to make scrumptious pies and cakes. My sister-in-law Mary Lampton Puckett makes a delicious apple cake, and when company's coming—especially in fall or winter—I turn to her recipe for a tried-and-true crowd-pleaser.

This festive fall menu is one I served for a seated dinner party last October to welcome a new member to my church. It featured some of my favorite fall foods as well as some old friends from my recipe collection. Warm Crab Dip and Savory Raspberry Pecan Cheesecake were set out as appetizers for guests to enjoy with a glass of wine as we gathered. Cooking with pecans always brings back loving memories of fall days spent with my grandfather. A giant pecan tree in my grandparents' backyard provided a sturdy limb for an old tire swing and an endless supply of tasty pecans. My grandfather carried a big basket for us to fill with pecans that had dropped to the ground. He and I would spend the afternoon on the back porch shelling the pecans that my grandmother made into a pie as our reward. She would carefully bag and freeze the leftover nuts to use in the months ahead. Like my grandmother, I always keep pecans in the freezer for recipes like this.

Crab dip is a traditional Southern favorite, and every Southern cook thinks her crab dip is the best. I suppose I'm no exception. Fresh lump crabmeat is a heavenly treat and undoubtedly my favorite food. I'm passing along my own recipe, which has been perfected through years of catering and entertaining in my home. It's a wonderful warm dip and can also be used as a side dish.

The centerpiece of the menu is a delicious make-ahead chicken and wild rice casserole from my mom's friend Jane Lewis. Jane was the first "real cook" I knew. She and her husband, Leon, lived a street over from our Bellewood Road home, and their back door and Jane's cookie jar were always open to the kids who roamed the neighborhood. There was always something delicious coming out of the oven, whether it was homemade bread, one of her special desserts, or a scrumptious casserole like this one.

No dinner party is complete in my home without the soft, buttery, fragrant dinner rolls made by my grandmother, Helen Todd. As her namesake, I knew it was up to me to carry on her roll-making tradition. For years I was deluded into thinking that something this heavenly just had to be hard, but I was so wrong. Making these rolls is incredibly easy and the rewards are more than worth the effort.

Helping Hands

Help from the Seasoned Cook

Peeling butternut squash requires basic knife skills. Grandmother's Dinner Rolls are no problem for a baker who knows how to work with yeast. The dough must be refrigerated overnight.

Help from the Kids

Pulling yellow or damaged leaves off Brussels sprouts is a task for little hands that can be a big help and time-saver. Kids can also crack eggs and sift ingredients for Lampton's Fresh Apple Cake.

Warm Crab Dip

2 tablespoons olive oil + oil for coating baking dish

1 onion, chopped

1 clove garlic, minced

1 pound lump crabmeat, picked through to remove any pieces of shell

1 cup canned artichoke hearts, drained and chopped

1 cup freshly grated Parmesan cheese

1 cup mayonnaise

½ cup fresh bread crumbs

2 tablespoons chopped green onions

2 tablespoons Worcestershire sauce

6 shakes Tabasco sauce

2 teaspoons Dijon mustard

Kosher salt and black pepper

Unsalted wafers or crackers for serving

Preheat the oven to 350°F. Lightly oil a 1-quart baking dish and set aside.

Heat olive oil in a large skillet over medium-high heat. Add onion and garlic and sauté until soft, 3 to 4 minutes.

Transfer to a large bowl and add crabmeat, artichokes, cheese, mayonnaise, bread crumbs, green onions, Worcestershire sauce, Tabasco sauce, mustard, salt, and pepper. Mix until thoroughly combined.

Scrape mixture into the prepared baking dish. Bake for 30 to 35 minutes, or until bubbling around the edges. Serve warm with wafers.

Makes 8 to 10 servings

Kitchen Note

- This dip can be served in a ramekin as a side dish, or as a first course. It would be great as a topping for fish or beef tenderloin.

Savory Raspberry Pecan Cheesecake

1 pound bacon, cooked and crumbled

1 pound Cheddar cheese, shredded

1 bunch green onions, chopped

¾ cup mayonnaise

1¼ cups finely chopped pecans

1 (10-ounce) jar seedless raspberry preserves

Unsalted wafers or crackers for serving

In a large bowl, combine bacon, cheese, green onions, mayonnaise, and 1 cup of the pecans.

Coat a 7-inch springform pan with cooking spray, then lightly wipe the pan with a paper towel. Spread mixture in the pan. Cover and refrigerate overnight.

Top the cheesecake with raspberry preserves followed by remaining ¼ cup pecans. Serve with wafers.

Makes 8 to 10 servings

Kitchen Note

- This tasty and impressive starter is very simple, but it must be made a day ahead.
- To shorten prep time, buy precooked bacon.

Autumn Salad

Vinaigrette

- ½ cup olive oil
- ¼ cup white wine vinegar
- 1 tablespoon Dijon mustard
- ½ teaspoon dried dill
- ½ teaspoon ground nutmeg
- ⅛ teaspoon salt
- ⅛ teaspoon black pepper

Salad

- 1 head romaine lettuce, washed, dried, and torn
- 1 bunch watercress, washed, dried, and stemmed
- 1 cup red seedless grapes, halved
- Ground nutmeg, to taste
- Salt and black pepper
- ⅓ cup crumbled Roquefort cheese
- ¼ cup walnuts

To make vinaigrette: Whisk all the vinaigrette ingredients together in a small bowl.

To make salad: Combine romaine, watercress, and grapes in a salad bowl.

Toss salad with vinaigrette.

Add nutmeg, salt, and pepper; taste and adjust seasonings.

Serve salad on individual plates sprinkled with Roquefort and walnuts.

Makes 8 servings

Kitchen Note

- Any autumnal food, such as apples or pecans, may be substituted for grapes.

Jane Lewis's Chicken and Wild Rice Casserole

1 onion, sliced

1 cup water

1 cup dry vermouth

1½ teaspoons salt

½ teaspoon curry powder

4 pounds boneless, skinless chicken breasts

2 (6-ounce) boxes long-grain and wild rice mix (such as Uncle Ben's)

½ cup unsalted butter

½ pound fresh mushrooms, stems removed, sliced

1 cup sour cream

3 tablespoons mayonnaise

1 (10¾-ounce) can condensed mushroom soup

Black pepper

1 cup Grape-Nuts cereal

½ cup slivered almonds

Preheat the oven 350°F. Butter a 3-quart casserole dish.

Bring onion, water, vermouth, salt, and curry powder to a boil in a large skillet. Add chicken, reduce heat, and gently poach until tender.

Cut chicken into bite-size pieces. Strain the cooking broth into a bowl and set aside.

Cook rice according to package directions, using the reserved broth and adding water to make the amount of liquid needed.

Melt ¼ cup butter in medium skillet. Add mushrooms and sauté until lightly browned.

Combine sour cream, mayonnaise, and mushroom soup in a large bowl. Fold in chicken, rice, mushrooms, and pepper.

Transfer mixture to the prepared casserole.

Melt remaining ¼ cup butter in a medium skillet. Stir in cereal and almonds. Sprinkle over casserole.

Bake casserole for 30 to 35 minutes, or until it is heated through and topping is lightly browned.

Makes 8 to 10 servings

Kitchen Note

- The casserole can be assembled a day ahead. Bring to room temperature before baking.

Roasted Brussels Sprouts with Apples

1½ pounds Brussels sprouts

1 tablespoon + 2 teaspoons good-quality olive oil

Kosher salt and black pepper

3 apples peeled, cored, and cut into 1-inch cubes

Preheat the oven to 400°F.

Cut off the ends of Brussels sprouts and discard any yellow outer leaves.

Mix sprouts in a large bowl with 1 tablespoon of the olive oil, ¾ teaspoon salt, and ½ teaspoon pepper.

Turn sprouts out onto a baking sheet. Roast, shaking the pan from time to time to brown the sprouts evenly, for 25 minutes, or until sprouts are crisp outside and tender inside.

Toss apples with remaining 2 teaspoons olive oil and season with salt and pepper.

Add apples to Brussels sprouts. Roast for 10 minutes longer, or until apples are softened.

Makes 8 servings

Kitchen Note

- If your Brussels sprouts are very large, cut them in half.

Oven-Baked Butternut Squash

2 large butternut squash

½ cup unsalted butter, melted

⅓ cup firmly packed light brown sugar

1 teaspoon kosher salt

½ teaspoon black pepper

1 cup toasted pecans (see Kitchen Notes, below)

Preheat the oven to 400°F.

Peel squash, cut each in half lengthwise, and remove the seeds. Cut into cubes and place in a large bowl.

Add butter, brown sugar, salt, and pepper. Toss well.

Spread in a single layer on a baking sheet. Roast, turning halfway through, for 40 to 50 minutes, or until the glaze begins to caramelize.

Transfer squash to a serving bowl, toss in pecans, and serve hot.

Makes 8 servings

Kitchen Notes

- **To toast pecans:** Preheat the oven to 300°F. Spread the pecans evenly on a baking sheet and bake, stirring often, for 10 to 15 minutes, or until the pecans are fragrant and lightly browned; do not overcook. Cool completely. You can make the toasted pecans in advance (in fact, make extra for future uses). The pecans can be stored in an airtight container in the freezer or refrigerator.

- You can also toast pecans in butter. For the method, see page 81.

Grandmother's Dinner Rolls

½ cup sugar

½ cup vegetable shortening

2 cups milk

1 (¼-ounce) package active dry yeast

¼ cup warm water (105°F–115°F)

4 cups all-purpose flour

1 teaspoon baking soda

1 teaspoon baking powder

1 teaspoon salt

Honey or butter

In a small saucepan, melt sugar and shortening in milk over low heat. Let cool.

In cup, dissolve yeast in warm water.

When milk mixture is cool, transfer to a large bowl and add yeast mixture and 2 cups of the flour. Beat with a hand mixer or wooden spoon to remove lumps.

Cover with a clean dish towel and let rise in a warm place until doubled in size, about 45 minutes.

In a large bowl, sift together 1½ cups of the remaining flour, the baking soda, baking powder, and salt.

Stir flour mixture into dough. Cover and refrigerate overnight.

Preheat the oven to 400°F. Grease 2 large baking sheets.

On floured board or countertop, work enough of the remaining ½ cup flour into sticky dough until it is the right consistency for rolling out.

With a floured rolling pin, roll out dough to a ½ inch thickness. Cut out rounds with a 2-inch biscuit cutter.

Fold rounds in half and place on the prepared sheets. Cover and let rise for 20 minutes.

Bake rolls for 10 to 12 minutes, or until lightly browned.

Serve warm with honey or butter.

Makes 3 to 4 dozen rolls

Kitchen Note

- You can prebake the rolls for 4 to 6 minutes at 400°F and freeze (do not let them brown). Thaw, then bake in a 400°F oven for 6 to 8 minutes, or until browned.

Lampton's Apple Cake

This is a winner any time of year.

Cake

1½ cups vegetable oil

2¼ cups granulated sugar

2 large eggs

2 teaspoons vanilla extract

3 cups all-purpose flour

1½ teaspoons baking soda

1 teaspoon ground cinnamon

1 teaspoon ground nutmeg

1 teaspoon salt

3 cups chopped peeled apples (in good-size chunks)

1 cup chopped nuts

Sauce

½ cup unsalted butter

½ cup firmly packed brown sugar

2 tablespoons milk

½ teaspoon vanilla extract

To make cake: Preheat the oven to 350°F. Grease and flour a Bundt pan.

In a large bowl, slowly mix together oil, granulated sugar, eggs, and vanilla.

In another large bowl, sift together flour, baking soda, cinnamon, nutmeg, and salt. Stir into oil mixture. Fold in apples and nuts.

Pour into the prepared pan. Bake for 1 hour and 15 minutes, or until golden.

To make sauce: In a medium saucepan, bring butter, brown sugar, and milk to a simmer and cook for 1 minute. Remove the pan from the heat and let mixture cool briefly.

Stir in vanilla.

Gently prick cake with a fork in a few places. Pour sauce over cake while the cake is still warm.

Makes 10 to 12 servings

Kitchen Notes

- Granny Smith apples are the best choice for this cake.

- To grease and flour the Bundt pan, rub the pan well with the butter or shortening, then sprinkle flour into the pan and tap, turn, and tilt to coat it well.

CHAPTER 7

Supper in the Kitchen

Summer Supper for 8 guests

Roasted Tomatoes and Garlic over Goat Cheese 75

Warm Garden Pasta with Shrimp, Smoked Mozzarella, and Fresh Basil 76

Butter Lettuce with Parmesan Dressing 78

Crusty French Bread 78

Leon's Fresh Blueberry Pie 79

Winter Supper for 8 guests

Baked Blue Cheese and Bacon Dip 80

Baked Asiago Cheese Dip 80

Spinach Salad with Cranberries and Toasted Pecans 81

Brunswick Stew 82

Fresh Green Beans with Caramelized Red Onions 84

Ruth King's Brownies 85

I call this menu *Supper in the Kitchen* because that's where everyone seems to gather at my house, even during a hot, humid Mississippi summer evening. With the thermometer on my back porch pushing a hundred degrees and the air conditioner straining to keep up, I wanted a summer supper that was delicious, colorful, and cool. I looked no further than my own backyard, where the basil was lush, and to the local farmers' market, with ripe red tomatoes from Crystal Springs. Crystal Springs, a small town about 30 miles down the road, is so renowned for its tomatoes that it calls itself the "tomatopolis" of the world. For my supper, I rooted through my refrigerator and found a piece of smoked mozzarella, the perfect accompaniment for the tomatoes and basil. The mozzarella was a gift from my dear friend and former employer, Paula Lambert of the Mozzarella Company in Dallas, which unquestionably makes some of the best cheeses on the planet. We've been friends for about 20 years, and I love to pick up the phone and order her award-winning cheeses, which are delivered the next day through the miracle of overnight shipping. I combined these ingredients to make a summer pasta salad that is not only tasty but makes a colorful presentation.

For a winter supper in the kitchen, nothing warms the bones on a cold night like a pot of my grandmother's Brunswick Stew. I ladle it into bowls over toasted garlic bread. Garlic bread is one of my teenage son's favorites, so I am always trying to find a way to do something different with it. Baked Blue Cheese and Bacon Dip is simply a warm, delicious dish to start the evening. Any blue cheese will do, but for a special treat I order Paula's Deep Ellum Blue. It's great for a dip like this or crumbled onto soup or into a salad. I like to set out a variety of dips in my kitchen because that's where everyone gathers while I'm putting the finishing touches on the meal. And I've found that guests love to help. It's fun for them and it makes having friends over easier for me. Late afternoons usually find me picking up my son from one of his various music lessons or school activities; so with everyone involved, it makes entertaining a cinch.

Recipes like Ruth King's Brownies live on long after the people who share them with us, and they evoke memories, tastes, and smells. As I was making these brownies last night, I thought of Ruth, an Auntie Mame–like character who started out as my Mom's interior decorator but became one of her dearest friends and a guiding presence in our lives. She was a true original, impeccably dressed with her hair in a bun that was always askew. She believed—whether working with a young couple on their first house, a college apartment, or a dream home—that whatever a person's financial circumstances, everyone should be "surrounded by beauty." She was larger than life to all of us and took seriously her reputation as a role model for all things beautiful and hospitable. She delighted in hosting mother/daughter breakfasts and would invite Mom and me along with my best friend, Mary Yerger, and her mother. Her house was full of treasures, and she always sent us home with something special. Once she gave Mary and me a plate of her special brownies to take to our less fortunate siblings who weren't invited to join us. I've asked my mother for years if she had the recipe for Ruth's brownies; but sometimes recipes, like memories, are packed away carefully and are not brought out to share lightly. When Mom finally gave me the recipe, I went straight to the market, got the ingredients, and went home to bake. The brownies I made are almost as good as hers, although there was one missing ingredient—her inimitable laughter.

Helping Hands

FOR THE SUMMER SUPPER
Help from the Seasoned Cook

Have a friend who enjoys cooking help you with the Roasted Tomatoes and Garlic over Goat Cheese and the Garden Pasta.

Help from the Kids

Kids can wash the blueberries for the pie, as well as roll the basil and cut the leaves with scissors for the pasta. Most kids enjoy tasks with detail so this is a fun activity for them.

FOR THE WINTER SUPPER
Help from the Seasoned Cook

The Brunswick Stew and Green Bean recipes are for an experienced cook. Basic cooking skills and kitchen techniques are needed.

Help from the Kids

Let the kids prepare garlic bread for the Brunswick Stew. Everyone loves making brownies and the kids can assist by cracking eggs, greasing the pan, and helping to measure. And of course they love to lick the bowl.

Roasted Tomatoes and Garlic over Goat Cheese

2 pints grape tomatoes, each cut in half

6 cloves garlic

Kosher salt

1 tablespoon red wine vinegar

1 tablespoon capers

¼ cup dried basil

Extra-virgin olive oil

1 (8-ounce) log goat cheese

Store-bought or homemade crostini (see Kitchen Notes, below)

Preheat the oven to 250°F. Coat a baking sheet with oil.

Place tomatoes cut side down on the baking sheet, along with garlic. Sprinkle with salt. Bake for 2 hours. Let cool briefly.

Place tomatoes and garlic in a jar with a lid.

Add vinegar, capers, and basil. Stir well.

Cover mixture with olive oil, cover the jar, and refrigerate overnight.

Bring tomato mixture to room temperature before serving. When ready to serve, place goat cheese log on a serving plate. Pour roasted tomato mixture over the log. Serve with crostini.

Makes 8 to 10 servings

Kitchen Notes

- For optimum flavor, you need to make this the day before.
- You can roast the tomatoes and garlic while you are prepping everything else for the supper.
- I also use small yellow tomatoes or a mix of both.
- To make your own crostini: With a serrated knife, cut a baguette into ¼-inch-thick slices. Place on a baking sheet and toast in a 400°F oven, turning once, for 5 to 6 minutes or until golden on both sides.

Warm Garden Pasta with Shrimp, Smoked Mozzarella, and Fresh Basil

6 large ripe tomatoes, cut into ½-inch cubes

1 pound smoked mozzarella, torn into irregular pieces

1¼ cups fresh basil leaves, rinsed, patted dry, and cut into strips

3 cloves garlic, finely minced

½ teaspoon salt

½ teaspoon black pepper

1 cup + 1 tablespoon good-quality olive oil

1½ pounds linguine

2 pounds medium shrimp, peeled, deveined, and cooked (about 40 shrimp)

Freshly grated Parmesan cheese

At least 2 hours before serving, combine tomatoes, mozzarella, basil, garlic, salt, and pepper in a large bowl. Stir in 1 cup of the olive oil. Let stand at room temperature.

In a large pot, bring 6 quarts of water to boil. Add the remaining 1 tablespoon olive oil and the linguine. Cook according to package directions until al dente.

Drain the pasta and immediately toss with tomato mixture and shrimp. Serve at once, sprinkled with cheese.

Makes 8 to 10 servings

Kitchen Notes

- Try the pasta with shredded rotisserie chicken instead of the shrimp.

- The shrimp can be cooked a day ahead and refrigerated. I like to sauté them briefly in a little olive oil rather than boiling them.

- To quickly cut basil into strips—also called chiffonade—pile up 5 or 6 leaves, then roll into a little "cigar." Cut across the roll to create thin strips.

Butter Lettuce with Parmesan Dressing

Parmesan Dressing

½ cup freshly grated Parmesan cheese

3 large eggs, at room temperature

¼ cup fresh lemon juice

1½ teaspoons minced garlic

1½ teaspoons Worcestershire sauce

¾ teaspoon white pepper

1 cup vegetable oil

Salad

3 heads Bibb lettuce, cut into quarters

Freshly grated Parmesan cheese

To make dressing: Combine Parmesan, eggs, lemon juice, garlic, Worcestershire, and pepper in a food processor. With the machine running, add oil in a thin stream until blended. The dressing will be smooth and pale. Cover and refrigerate until ready to use.

To make salad: Divide lettuce wedges among 8 chilled salad plates. Spoon dressing over lettuce and toss lightly to coat the leaves. Sprinkle with Parmesan and serve.

Makes 8 servings

Kitchen Note

- If you prefer not to use raw eggs in the dressing, coddle them: Let the eggs sit for 1 minute in 2 cups of water that has been boiled and removed from the heat, then remove the eggs and use. Or you could try some plain yogurt instead, but it will change the flavor of the dressing.

Crusty French Bread

¾ cup unsalted butter, melted

2 teaspoons chopped green onion

2 teaspoons lemon juice

2 teaspoons Dijon mustard

2 teaspoons poppy seeds

2 teaspoons kosher salt

1 clove garlic, minced

1 loaf po' boy bread or French bread

1 cup grated Italian blend cheese

Paprika

Preheat the oven to 350°F. In a medium bowl, combine butter, green onion, lemon juice, mustard, poppy seeds, salt, and garlic. Mix well.

Slice bread and brush slices with butter mixture. Top with grated cheese and sprinkle with a little paprika.

Bake for 8 to 10 minutes or until cheese is melted.

Makes 8 servings

Leon's Fresh Blueberry Pie

Each August, Leon Lewis joins my parents and their good friends Gus and Jonelle Primos and Jimmy and Sudie Manning for a Maine holiday. They rent a big rambling house overlooking the sea, and spend their days exploring the countryside and their nights cooking for each other. Each person is assigned a night to cook. When it's Leon's turn, this delicious Blueberry Pie made with fresh wild Maine blueberries will always be on the menu.

¾ cup sugar

2 tablespoons all-purpose flour

½ teaspoon salt

4½ cups blueberries

1 tablespoon lemon juice

2 (9-inch) pie crusts (see The Best Pie Crust, page 194)

Unsalted butter to dot on top of berries

Preheat the oven to 425°F. Spray a 9-inch pie pan with nonstick spray, then wipe the pan lightly with a paper towel.

Mix sugar, flour, and salt in a large bowl.

Add berries and lemon juice. Set aside for 10 minutes.

Fit one of the dough rounds into the pie pan. Spoon berry mixture into pie shell. Dot with butter.

Place other dough round on top and crimp edges to seal. Cut two or three slits in the top crust. Bake for 30 minutes; reduce the heat to 350°F.

Continue to bake for about 10 minutes until the crust browns.

Makes 8 servings

Kitchen Notes

- The pie filling is a little loose. This is more like a cobbler.
- Serve in a bowl with a scoop of vanilla ice cream on top

Baked Blue Cheese and Bacon Dip

8 slices bacon, chopped

3 cloves garlic, minced

8 ounces cream cheese, softened

¼ cup half-and-half

4 ounces blue cheese, crumbled (1 cup)

2 tablespoons chopped fresh chives

Preheat the oven to 350°F.

Cook bacon in a large skillet over medium heat until almost crisp, about 5 minutes. Drain excess fat from the skillet.

Add garlic and cook until bacon is crisp, about 2 minutes.

Beat cream cheese until smooth in a medium bowl. Add half-and-half and mix until combined.

Stir in bacon mixture, blue cheese, and chives.

Transfer to a 2-cup ovenproof serving dish and cover with foil. Bake for about 30 minutes, or until thoroughly heated through.

Makes 8 servings

Kitchen Notes

- Serve with plain crackers.
- The dish can be assembled a day in advance; cover and refrigerate. Bring to room temperature before baking.

Baked Asiago Cheese Dip

1 cup mayonnaise

1 cup sour cream

1 cup shredded Asiago cheese

¼ cup chopped mushrooms, sautéed in butter

¼ cup sun-dried tomatoes packed in oil, drained and chopped

2 green onions, green parts only, sliced

½ teaspoon minced garlic

Preheat the oven to 350°F.

In a medium bowl, blend mayonnaise, sour cream, and ½ cup of the cheese. Fold in mushrooms, tomatoes, green onions, and garlic.

Pour mixture into a loaf pan. Sprinkle remaining ½ cup cheese on top.

Bake for 20 minutes, or until bubbly. Transfer to a serving bowl and serve warm.

Makes 8 servings

Spinach Salad with Cranberries and Toasted Pecans

Dressing

¼ cup olive oil

¼ cup seasoned rice vinegar

2 tablespoons chopped fresh parsley

¾ teaspoon Dijon mustard

½ teaspoon prepared horseradish

1 medium clove garlic, crushed

Salad

1 cup pecan halves

1 tablespoon unsalted butter

2 (10-ounce) bags spinach, washed and spun dry

1 (11-ounce) can mandarin oranges, drained

1 pint grape tomatoes, cut in half lengthwise

½ cup dried cranberries

½ cup crumbled goat cheese

To make dressing: Whisk olive oil, vinegar, parsley, mustard, horseradish, and garlic in a small bowl or process in a food processor until smooth. Cover and refrigerate until ready to serve.

To make salad: Sauté pecans in butter in a medium skillet over medium heat until toasted.

Combine spinach, oranges, tomatoes, and cranberries in a large bowl and toss to mix.

Pour dressing over spinach mixture and toss to coat.

Sprinkle with toasted pecans and cheese. Serve immediately.

Makes 8 servings

Brunswick Stew

½ to 1 cup all-purpose flour

Salt and black pepper

2 pounds boneless beef chuck, cut into 1-inch cubes

½ cup olive oil (approximately)

½ cup chopped onion

3 cups beef broth

3 cups canned tomatoes

1 tablespoon Worcestershire sauce

2 teaspoons sugar

¼ teaspoon cayenne pepper

1½ cups whole kernel corn (fresh, frozen, or canned)

1½ cups lima beans (fresh, frozen, or canned)

1 pound button mushrooms, stems removed, thickly sliced

3 tablespoons unsalted butter

Garlic bread (page 171)

In a shallow bowl, season flour with 1 tablespoon salt and 1 tablespoon pepper.

Dredge beef cubes in the flour to coat.

Heat 2 tablespoons of the olive oil in a large Dutch oven over medium-high heat. In batches, and adding more oil as necessary, sauté beef until browned. Transfer to a plate and set aside.

Add onion to pan and cook, stirring occasionally, until translucent, about 5 minutes.

Stir in broth, tomatoes, Worcestershire, sugar, and cayenne.

Return beef to pot. Cover and simmer until beef is almost tender, about 1½ hours.

Add corn and lima beans. Continuing cooking until vegetables are tender, about 20 minutes.

In a medium pan, sauté mushrooms in butter, until lightly browned, about 10 minutes. Add to stew.

Bring the stew to a boil, reduce the heat, and simmer, uncovered, until thickened slightly, about 15 minutes. Serve hot in individual bowls over a slice of toasted garlic bread.

Makes 8 servings

Kitchen Note

● As an alternative to garlic bread, serve the stew over cooked long-grain white rice.

Brunswick Stew (opposite) and
Garlic Bread (page 171)

Fresh Green Beans
with Caramelized Red Onions

2 pounds fresh green beans, trimmed

2 large red onions, cut in half and thinly sliced

2 tablespoons unsalted butter

2 teaspoons fresh thyme leaves, chopped

1½ teaspoons salt

½ teaspoon black pepper

Fill a large bowl with ice water; set aside. Bring a 6- to 8-quart pot of salted water to a boil.

Add beans to the boiling water and cook for 4 minutes, or until crisp-tender. With a slotted spoon or strainer, transfer beans to the bowl of ice water and let cool. Drain thoroughly.

In nonstick skillet, combine onions, butter, thyme, salt, and pepper. Cook over medium heat, stirring occasionally, until onions start to brown, about 15 minutes. Reduce heat to medium-low and cook, stirring frequently, until onions turn dark brown, 5 to 7 minutes longer.

Stir beans into onion mixture. Heat through, stirring frequently.

Makes 8 servings

Kitchen Notes

- To trim green beans, snap off the ends and remove the strings. Keep an eye out for the stringless varieties.

- Frozen green beans are a perfectly acceptable substitute for fresh ones.

Variation

Green Beans with Lemon Thyme Butter: Skip the onions and in the skillet combine the butter, the zest of 1 lemon, 2 teaspoons of lemon thyme, and salt and pepper to taste. Add the prepared beans and heat through.

Ruth King's Brownies

Brownies

2 cups all-purpose flour

2 cups granulated sugar

½ teaspoon salt

1 cup water

½ cup unsalted butter

½ cup vegetable shortening

3 tablespoons unsweetened cocoa powder

½ cup buttermilk

2 large eggs

1 tablespoon vanilla extract

1 teaspoon baking soda

Icing

1 (16-ounce) box confectioners' sugar

1 cup chopped nuts

½ cup unsalted butter

6 tablespoons unsweetened cocoa powder

6 tablespoons whole milk

1 teaspoon vanilla extract

To make brownies: Preheat the oven to 350°F. Grease and flour a 10- by 15-inch baking pan.

In a large bowl, mix flour, granulated sugar, and salt.

In a medium saucepan, bring water, butter, shortening, and cocoa to a boil. Stir into dry ingredients.

Add buttermilk, eggs, vanilla, and baking soda and mix well.

Pour into prepared pan. Bake for 20 minutes, or until a toothpick inserted in the center comes out clean.

To make icing: Place confectioners' sugar, nuts, butter, cocoa powder, milk, and vanilla in a medium saucepan. Cook, over medium heat stirring, until melted. Do not boil! Pour over warm brownies.

Makes 2 dozen brownies

CHAPTER 8

Teen Taco Bar

for 6 guests

It's true. One morning you wake up and your child has been transformed overnight into a teenager. These newly minted teenagers seem to change everything about themselves from hair and clothes to attitude and even taste buds. Lately, I find myself with teenagers in and out of my house constantly and, no matter what the time of day, they always seem to be hungry.

So it was with appropriate apprehension that I spent a weeklong vacation with a group of teenagers all under one roof. My son, Martin, his friend Duncan, and I shared a rambling house in Seaside, Florida, last summer with our friends Marsha and Tim Cannon. Their teenage daughter Clara Frances had her friend Mary Christopher in tow. Feeding a house full of teenagers on summer vacation called for planning, a sense of humor, and a laid-back attitude. We fed them a hearty breakfast before sending them off for the day's activities, with lunch on their own and a casual dinner at the house each night. Our mantra was "keep it simple." After all, grown-ups need a holiday too. One sunny morning Martin, Duncan, Clara Frances, and Mary Christopher surprised us when they announced the need for money to buy groceries, as they planned to cook for their friends.

I immediately started giving advice, only to be firmly reminded that they didn't need my help. All of these kids had been students in my cooking classes, so they knew their way around the kitchen. They planned and prepared a delicious dinner with pork tenderloin and all the trimmings. It was a humbling reminder that teens have more sense than we sometimes think. They'll avoid the allure of fast food if offered a tasty alternative, and inviting them as active participants in the family kitchen will reap future dividends.

Impressed with their enthusiasm and kitchen skills, I challenged the gang of four to come up with their own menu for this book, and the result was a taco party. It reflects their sense of fun and creativity, not to mention the tastes and textures they love. And the menu is not just for teenagers, but is festive party fare to be enjoyed by all ages.

The idea of the taco bar is for each diner to create a custom concoction using favorite ingredients. A variety of meats, cheeses, condiments, and toppings should be set out in decorative bowls and cups, and the teens can do the rest. Quesadillas are easy to make, fun to eat, and everyone always clamors for seconds. During my catering days in Dallas, these quesadillas were such a hit they were featured in the *Dallas Morning News*. To make them, I use three cheeses and spinach, or whatever vegetable might be on hand. Teens will eat spinach on quesadillas—especially if they are the ones who make them.

Duncan loves peaches, so he and I came up with a recipe for peach salsa, which can also serve as a savory, spicy accompaniment for fish. Queso is one of my son, Martin's, favorite foods and his version has just the right kick to it. It's good as an after-school snack or a party dip; it isn't the familiar processed-cheese queso, but made with a combination of Colby and Monterey Jack cheeses. Clara Frances and Mary Christopher came up with the unusual version of s'mores, featuring a flour tortilla sprinkled with marshmallows and chocolate chips. The tortilla is folded in half or topped with another, brushed with butter, and sprinkled with cinnamon sugar. These delightful treats live up to their name, as everyone always comes back for "some more."

The final tip from Martin and friends is that they enjoyed preparing the meal themselves. It's a polite way of telling me and other parents to stay out of the kitchen. Besides providing groceries, serving pieces, and a little advice, parents don't need to tell teens what to do in the kitchen, and they certainly would prefer that we don't. As parents of teens we grudgingly learn that sometimes they do just fine without us.

Helping Hands

Help from the Seasoned Cook

Adults can take a break with this menu and invite the seasoned teen cook to peel, chop, and dice ingredients for the Peach Salsa and tacos.

Help from the Kids

Allow your young friends to make the Mexican S'Mores. They'll enjoy sprinkling on the chocolate chips and marshmallows and brushing the tortillas with butter.

Martin's Queso

1 tablespoon vegetable oil

1 small onion, minced

2 cloves garlic, minced

2 jalapeño chiles, minced

1 (10-ounce) can Rotel diced tomatoes and green chilies, with liquid

½ pound Colby Longhorn cheese, cubed

½ pound Monterey Jack cheese, cubed

Tortilla chips or cut-up vegetables

Heat oil in a medium saucepan over medium heat and sauté onion, garlic, and jalapeños until softened. Add tomatoes and their liquid and cook for about 5 minutes to reduce the liquid.

When tomatoes begin to look dry, reduce the heat to medium-low and start adding Colby and Jack cheeses a handful at a time, stirring until cheeses melt (wait for each handful to melt before adding more cheese).

Serve in a chafing dish or fondue pot to keep queso warm. Offer tortilla chips or cut-up vegetables for dipping.

Makes 6 servings

Peach Salsa

2 tablespoons honey

2 tablespoons fresh lime juice

2 cups diced peeled yellow peaches

¼ cup diced red bell pepper

¼ cup diced green bell pepper

¼ cup diced yellow bell pepper

¼ cup diced English or hothouse cucumber

¼ cup sliced green onions (cut on bias)

1 to 2 fresh jalapeño chiles, seeded and minced, to taste

2 teaspoons chopped fresh cilantro

Pinch sea salt

Chips for dipping

In a large bowl, combine honey and lime juice and mix well.

Add peaches, bell peppers, cucumber, green onions, jalapeños, cilantro, and salt.

Cover and chill up to 4 hours, stirring once or twice. Serve with chips for dipping.

Makes 2½ cups

Build-Your-Own Tacos

Meat Filling

2 pounds ground beef or cubed boneless skinless chicken breast

2 tablespoons chili powder

2 tablespoons paprika

1 teaspoon ground cumin

1 teaspoon garlic powder or ground cloves

1 teaspoon salt

½ medium onion, diced

Taco Bar

12 taco shells

Chopped green onions

Shredded lettuce

Chopped tomatoes

Chopped fresh cilantro

Sliced avocado

Lime wedges

Assortment of favorite shredded cheese

Sour cream

To make meat filling: Combine beef or chicken, chili powder, paprika, cumin, garlic powder, salt, and enough water to cover meat in a 2-quart saucepan. Bring to a boil.

Reduce the heat, cover, and simmer over medium heat until thickened, about 45 minutes.

Stir in onion and cook for 20 to 30 minutes longer.

To heat shells and assemble taco bar: Preheat the oven to 300°F.

Place taco shells on a baking sheet and bake for 3 to 5 minutes, or until crisp.

Place the meat filling and condiments in separate bowls.

Have guests fill taco shells to their liking.

Makes 6 servings

Kitchen Notes

- You can use diced fish, pork, or grilled shrimp instead of the beef or chicken filling. For vegetarians, try refried black beans.

- The meat filling can be made a day ahead.

- Sliced avocado should be tossed with lemon or lime juice to prevent discoloration.

Triple-Cheese Quesadillas

1 (10-ounce) package frozen chopped spinach or 1 pound fresh spinach, cleaned and stemmed

2 tablespoons unsalted butter

1 medium onion, chopped

1 clove garlic, minced

½ cup prepared salsa

½ cup sour cream

12 flour tortillas

4 ounces sharp Cheddar cheese, shredded

4 ounces pepper Jack cheese, shredded

4 ounces mozzarella cheese, shredded

Vegetable oil for coating skillet

If using frozen spinach, thaw and drain.

In a large skillet, melt butter over medium-high heat. Add onion and garlic and sauté until softened.

Add spinach and sauté until wilted, 4 to 5 minutes. If using fresh spinach, drain well after sautéing. Transfer to a large bowl.

Stir in salsa and sour cream.

Divide spinach mixture equally among 6 tortillas and spread out.

Blend cheeses in a small bowl, then divide over spinach. Top with remaining tortillas and press down.

Cook quesadillas, one at a time, in a hot oiled skillet over medium heat. Cook on one side until lightly browned, then turn and cook on other side until tortilla is lightly browned and cheese is melted.

Cut each quesadilla into 6 wedges to serve.

Makes 6 servings

Kitchen Notes

- The quesadillas may be prepared in advance and held for an hour. To reheat, place on baking sheets in a single layer and heat in a 300°F oven until warm.

- Most markets carry a large array of prepared salsas from hot to mild. We prefer salsas refrigerated in plastic tubs for their fresher taste and texture.

- These quesadillas make a great appetizer for any gathering.

Easy Refried Beans

2 tablespoons olive oil

1 medium onion, chopped

½ medium green bell pepper, seeded and chopped

1 to 2 cloves garlic, minced, to taste

1 (18-ounce) can refried beans (preferably black beans, but red beans can be used)

1 teaspoon ground cumin

Salt and black pepper

Sour cream

Heat oil in a medium saucepan over medium heat. Add onion, bell pepper, and garlic and sauté until wilted, 3 to 5 minutes.

Add refried beans, stirring well to combine.

Add cumin and salt and pepper to taste and simmer briefly.

Serve topped with dollops of sour cream.

Makes 6 servings

Mexican S'Mores

6 (8- to 10-inch) flour tortillas

9 large marshmallows, cut in half, or 36 mini marshmallows

6 tablespoons milk chocolate chips

6 tablespoons unsalted butter, melted

Cinnamon sugar for sprinkling

Preheat the oven to 350°F. Line a large baking sheet with parchment paper.

Lay a tortilla flat. Sprinkle 3 large marshmallow halves or 6 mini marshmallows and 1 tablespoon chocolate chips on one-half of tortilla.

Fold over tortilla. Brush top with 1 tablespoon melted butter. Sprinkle with cinnamon sugar.

Repeat with remaining tortillas.

Place on prepared baking sheet and bake for 10 minutes, or until lightly browned.

Makes 6 s'mores

Kitchen Note

- You can purchase commercial cinnamon sugar or make your own by combining 1 part cinnamon to 3 parts sugar.

CHAPTER 9

Cookout Under the Stars at Blackberry Farm

for 8 guests

I met Kreis Beall while hiking a rocky trail in the Santa Monica Mountains. We were both participants in a wellness retreat, taking an important time-out from our hectic schedules to focus on our bodies and our lives. The most rewarding gift from my mountaintop experience was the gift of her friendship, as she became not only my friend but also my mentor. Through the years she has challenged me and shown me by her example to recognize and seize opportunities. When she asked me to create a cooking program for Blackberry Farm, her renowned luxury inn in Tennessee, I repeatedly asked her to share with me exactly what she wanted. Her gracious answer was this, "You have a master's degree in education and you're a teacher. You're the expert, not me. I'll tell you what I think after you've finished." When I completed my first Camp Blackberry series of cooking classes, I asked her what she thought and was pleased when she asked, "You're coming back, aren't you?"

Since then, my son, Martin, and I have spent major holidays in the enchanting Smoky Mountains of Tennessee, teaching cooking classes at Blackberry Farm. One of my favorite classes is Cookout Under the Stars. Gathering around the old stone fire pit, with the mountains in the distance bathed in moonlight, is a fantastic way to engage children in cooking. Whether a hot summer night or a cold winter evening, this menu works anytime of year at Blackberry Farm—or in your own backyard. Some foods can be prepped earlier in the day or even the day before so the entire family can get involved. At Blackberry, some kids help prepare the table while others gather around the fire pit cooking Hobo Packs and stirring the beans. There is always a task for everyone.

Clara's Corn Dip comes from my student Clara Frances Cannon, who started assisting me with classes when she was 12. Onion Sauté Surprise is the creation of Kreis Beall's granddaughter Cameron and is a tasty make-ahead side dish for any gathering. Cameron, who is also known at Blackberry Farm as Teensy, as I noted in Chapter 3, thoughtfully presented her recipe for Onion Sauté Surprise to me and everyone in her family as a Christmas gift. Made ahead, it's a tasty accompaniment to Hobo Packs. Most children love trail mix; it's a nutritious energy booster and a popular treat for a cookout or an after-school snack. This extraordinary version of trail mix was inspired by two other

Beall grandchildren, Sam and Rose, and is a simple variation on the Blackberry Farmhouse Cereal found in Chapter 1.

Make-Your-Own "Hobo Packs" are customary on Martin's Boy Scout campouts and are the perfect campfire fare. Everyone loves creating their own and personalizing them with favorite foods. Baked Beans are cooked over the fire from start to finish, with bacon and brown sugar intensifying the flavor of the beans. A Cookout Under the Stars would not be complete without a Blackberry Farm S'More. Making s'mores around the fire pit is a year-round Blackberry Farm tradition enjoyed by grown-ups and kids. Guests who wander out to the blazing fire will find long sticks cut and sharpened to toast marshmallows and a basket of s'more supplies. Individual bags are filled with the ingredients for one s'more—a graham cracker, one half of a chocolate bar, and a marshmallow—and guests are invited to make their own. The Beall children's clever variation is to make a batch of Teensy's Chocolate Chip Treats (page 28) and use them in place of a graham cracker. Everyone will want "some more" of this delicious dessert.

Helping Hands

Help from the Seasoned Cook

The seasoned cook can prep the meat and vegetables for the hobo packs, as well as build the fire.

Help from the Kids

Kids will enjoy preparing Campfire Corn by wrapping the corn in foil. They can also prep and make s'mores and have fun toasting the marshmallows.

Clara's Corn Dip

"I was nine years old when I first created this delicious dip. It is a favorite of young and old; it's perfect for school functions, tailgating events or a gathering of friends."

–Clara Frances Cannon

1 (11-ounce) can white shoepeg corn (small kerneled white corn), drained

1 cup shredded Cheddar cheese

½ cup shredded Parmesan cheese

1 bunch green onions, chopped

2 tablespoons chopped seeded fresh jalapeño chiles

2 tablespoons mayonnaise

Morton Nature's seasoning blend, to taste

Fritos Scoops corn chips for dipping

Combine corn, Cheddar cheese, Parmesan cheese, green onions, jalapeños, mayonnaise, and seasoning blend in a serving bowl and stir very well.

Serve with corn chips.

Makes 8 to 10 servings

Kitchen Note

- The dip can be made up to a day ahead and stored, covered, in the refrigerator.

Sam and Rose's Toasted Trail Mix

"We love making this with Ms. Helen. It is really yummy to us."

–Sam and Rose Beall

Blackberry Farmhouse Cereal (page 8)

1 cup M&Ms

½ cup milk chocolate chips

½ cup white chocolate chips

Toss all ingredients in a large bowl.

Serve in a decorative pail, or wrap individual servings in bandannas.

Makes 8 servings

Kitchen Notes

- You may include your favorite dried fruits and candies.
- In a pinch, substitute purchased granola for the cereal.

Make-Your-Own "Hobo Packs"

The great thing about hobo packs, as their name implies, is that you can use whatever herbs and vegetables you like. See the Kitchen Note, below, for some additional possibilities. These packs cook directly on the hot coals, so make sure your fire has burned down evenly.

4 carrots, thinly sliced into rounds

2 red bell peppers, seeded and cut into ½-inch-thick strips

2 yellow bell peppers, seeded and cut into ½-inch-thick strips

6 red potatoes, cut into ¼-inch-thick rounds

About 3 tablespoons olive oil

2 to 3 pounds boneless, skinless chicken tenders

Vegetable oil for coating foil

8 sprigs fresh thyme

Salt and black pepper

8 teaspoons Worcestershire sauce

Cut 16 (10- by 10-inch) pieces of heavy-duty aluminum foil. Bring a large pot of water to a boil.

Blanch carrots, peppers, and potatoes separately in the boiling water for 1 minute (remove with a slotted spoon) and drain well. Place vegetables in individual bowls.

Heat olive oil in a large skillet over medium-high heat and sauté chicken until lightly browned, 2 to 4 minutes; do not overcook. Transfer chicken to a bowl.

For each hobo pack: Lightly coat a sheet of the foil with oil. Have a guest mound his or her choice of vegetables and chicken in the center of the foil. Sprinkle with salt and pepper and 1 teaspoon of Worcestershire. Add a sprig of thyme. Toss to combine. Top with another piece of foil. Fold up the edges of the foil to seal the pack.

Place packs, folded edges up, directly on top of the hot coals. Cook for 20 minutes, then open one pack to check for doneness. Continue to cook, if necessary.

Remove from the coals and allow guests to carefully open their own packs.

Makes 8 servings

Kitchen Note

- Fennel or celery would work well instead of peppers and you can replace the red potatoes with sweet potato.

Cameron's Onion Sauté Surprise

"When I make it, my whole family loves it. My parents like it because it's healthy. . . . I like it because it's delicious. And I can bring it to the campfire. You can too."

—Cameron Beall

3 tablespoons olive oil

1 medium yellow onion, cut into medium dice

3½ tablespoons unsalted butter

Kosher salt and black pepper

2 to 3 cups fresh green beans, trimmed and cut 1 inch long

8 ounces cremini mushrooms, stems removed, cut into medium dice

½ cup chopped walnuts

2 to 3 cloves garlic, chopped

¾ teaspoon ground cinnamon

½ teaspoon dried basil

3 teaspoons brown sugar

Heat olive oil in a large skillet over medium heat. Add onion and sauté until softened, about 7 minutes. Add 2 tablespoons of the butter.

Sprinkle a pinch of salt and pepper over onions, then add green beans and mushrooms. Stir for a minute, reduce the heat to medium low, and cook until softened, 2 to 3 minutes.

Stir in walnuts and ½ tablespoon of the butter and cook for 2 minutes longer. Add garlic, cinnamon, basil, 1½ teaspoons of the brown sugar, the remaining 1 tablespoon butter, ½ teaspoon salt, and ¼ teaspoon pepper. Stir to incorporate all ingredients.

Add remaining 1½ teaspoons brown sugar, cook for 3 minutes longer, and *Voilà!* It's ready!

Makes 8 servings

Kitchen Note

● This tastes great on its own, with pasta, or as an accompaniment to sausage, chicken, or steak.

Over-the-Fire Baked Beans

3 slices bacon, diced

1 medium onion, finely chopped

3 (14.5-ounce) cans pork and beans

1 cup lightly packed brown sugar

½ cup ketchup

2 tablespoons prepared mustard

2 tablespoons Worcestershire sauce

3 shakes Tabasco sauce

Cook bacon over the fire in a Dutch oven until well cooked. Transfer to paper towels, leaving all the fat in the pan.

Add onion and cook, stirring, until translucent, about 7 minutes.

Add pork and beans and stir well.

Stir in brown sugar, ketchup, mustard, Worcestershire, and Tabasco.

Cook, uncovered, for 30 to 45 minutes, stirring to keep from sticking, or until piping hot.

Crumble bacon and use as garnish.

Makes 8 servings

Kitchen Note

- If you want to cook ahead, simmer uncovered on the stove for 2 hours. Then place over the fire until heated through.

Campfire Corn

Once the corn is off the fire, have each guest shuck an ear and add butter and salt and pepper, if desired. The corn is also delicious with Roasted Garlic Butter or Sun-Dried Tomato Butter (see Kitchen Notes, below).

8 unshucked ears fresh corn on the cob

8 tablespoons unsalted butter, softened

Kosher salt and black pepper

Wrap unshucked corn in foil. Place along the side of the grill rack, away from direct heat.

Grill, turning every 15 minutes, for 45 minutes. (The silk will steam to the husks, so when the foil is removed the corn will slip right out.)

Pass the butter and salt and pepper.

Makes 8 servings

Kitchen Notes

- For faster cooking, wrap unshucked corn in a paper towel and microwave for 7 minutes, then grill for 20 to 25 minutes, turning occasionally.

- **To make Roasted Garlic Butter:** Preheat the oven to 400°F. Cut off the top third of an entire head of garlic. Place the head, cut side up, on a piece of aluminum foil large enough to enclose it. Drizzle some olive oil over the top, and seal the head inside the foil. Roast for 25 minutes, or until the cloves are softened. Unwrap, let cool slightly, then squeeze the garlic from their papery sheaths into a small bowl. Add butter and mix with a fork until blended.

- **To make Sun-Dried Tomato Butter:** In a food processor, combine 2 sticks of softened unsalted butter, 3 large oil-packed sun-dried tomatoes (drained and finely chopped), 2 tablespoons finely chopped green onions, 2 minced garlic cloves, and kosher salt and freshly ground black pepper to taste. Process until well blended. Spoon butter into a crock or roll it into a log and chill, covered, for at least 2 hours.

Blackberry Farm S'Mores

4 Hershey's milk chocolate bars, broken
   into halves

8 marshmallows

8 graham crackers, broken into halves

Place a chocolate bar half on a graham cracker half.

Have guests toast marshmallow over the campfire (see Kitchen Notes) or over the flame of a gas grill.

Carefully place a toasted marshmallow on chocolate.

Top with second graham cracker half; gently press together.

Repeat to make additional s'mores.

Makes 8 s'mores

Kitchen Notes

- Before toasting your marshmallows, let the fire die down a bit. Marshmallows are best toasted over glowing embers rather than a flame.

- Make Teensy's Chocolate Chip Treats (page 28) and use the cookies instead of graham crackers.

- For passing around easy single servings by the fire, place 1 graham cracker, half a chocolate bar, and 1 marshmallow in individual zip-top bags.

CHAPTER 10

Everybody's Birthday Party

for 8 guests

My sister, Carol, loves a birthday party, not only for herself but also for everybody. She thinks everyone needs and deserves a birthday party and she is always happy to whip up one on short notice. Because of her demanding career and travel schedule, pulling together a party on a moment's notice is a product of necessity and not preference. Carol believes that being busy with work is no excuse for not living life to the fullest, especially when it comes to celebrating the birthdays of close friends and family.

With Carol, dessert comes first. The cake is always the centerpiece of her parties, and baking a mouthwatering birthday cake is where she spends her pre-party energy. Although the food is always delicious, it plays second fiddle to the cake. Carol started baking carrot cakes when she moved into her first apartment after college. Over the years she has experimented with numerous cake pans, different ways of shredding the carrots, and various versions of the recipe. Her most recent favorite is from Sara Foster's book, *The Foster's Market Cookbook*.

I have watched in awe as Carol spends hours baking a cake, quickly sets a table with treasures from her travels to Asia, then orders Chinese takeout. For Carol, the party is about setting a festive mood, then having fun with her friends. If she doesn't have time to cook, it doesn't deter her from having a party. Often her parties have a theme—like the pasta party she hosted for my father and his friends on his 77th birthday. Guests could choose from a buffet with two kinds of lasagna (ground turkey and artichoke and mushroom), spaghetti and meatballs, or whole-wheat pasta with homemade pesto. The tables were decorated with flowers in vases of empty cans of Italian tomatoes and various exotic ingredients. There have been Thai birthday parties and Vietnamese celebrations reflecting her love of Asian cuisine. But the best party of all was the one you'll find in this chapter—the one she hosted for me.

The evening began with two hors d'oeuvres, a tasty Sun-Dried Tomato Pesto Torta placed on the island in the kitchen for those who congregated while Carol put the finishing touches on our meal. Marvelous Mushroom Dip, an old standby and crowd-pleaser, accompanied the torta. The torta is made in a small springform pan that holds the layers of basil pesto and sun-dried tomato pesto. It's perfect for a party because you can make it ahead and pull it out of the refrigerator when it's time to serve. Because there are so many strong tastes in the torta, Carol uses plain crackers as an accompaniment.

A delicious seafood casserole with my favorite foods—eggplant, shrimp, and crabmeat—was the main course. Roasted tomatoes and a lemony salad added color and a refreshing counterpoint to the creamy casserole. Fresh crabmeat is not available everywhere, so frozen or canned can be substituted. I know that fresh crabmeat is expensive and usually reserved for special occasions, but I understand the high price because I've painstakingly picked many a crab. The party ended with the sounds of "Happy Birthday" and the serving of the carrot cake, of course. Everybody enjoys a birthday party!

Helping Hands

Help from the Seasoned Cook

The Shrimp and Eggplant Casserole requires an experienced palate to adjust the seasonings. If one of your friends loves to bake, have them make the carrot cake; the results are well worth the time and effort.

Help from the Kids

Let the kids tear the lettuce for the salad. They excel with a whisk, so let them whisk the dressing while you add the oil.

Sun-Dried Tomato Pesto Torta

2 (8-ounce) packages cream cheese, at room temperature

1 large egg

1 tablespoon Worcestershire sauce

2 drops Tabasco sauce

Dash salt

¾ cup sun-dried tomato pesto, drained to remove some of the oil

¾ cup basil pesto

¾ cup sour cream

1 teaspoon all-purpose flour

Baby lettuce leaves for serving

Unsalted wafers or crackers for serving

Preheat the oven to 325°F. Lightly butter a 7-inch springform pan.

In a large bowl, beat cream cheese with an electric mixer until softened.

Add egg, Worcestershire, Tabasco, and salt, beating on low speed until combined; divide cheese mixture into thirds.

Spread one-third of the cheese mixture into the prepared pan, spreading evenly. Top with sun-dried tomato pesto, spreading evenly to edge.

Spread another one-third cheese mixture over the tomato pesto and then top with basil pesto, spreading evenly to edge.

Spread the remaining cream cheese mixture over the basil pesto.

Place the pan on a baking sheet to catch drips. Bake for 15 minutes, or until set.

Stir together sour cream and flour in a small bowl; carefully spread over torta. Bake 5 minutes longer, or until set.

Cool to room temperature, then cover and chill for a minimum of 6 hours and up to 24 hours.

Remove side of pan. Serve on a bed of baby lettuce leaves with wafers.

Makes 8 servings

Kitchen Note

- This is supereasy to prepare, but keep in mind that it needs to chill for at least 6 hours.

Marvelous Mushroom Dip

1 pound mushrooms, coarsely chopped

½ cup chopped green onions

2 tablespoons chopped fresh parsley

1 teaspoon minced garlic

2 tablespoons unsalted butter

8 ounces cream cheese, softened

4 ounces sour cream

2 shakes Tabasco sauce

Garlic salt, to taste

Toast points for serving

In a large skillet, sauté mushrooms, green onions, parsley, and garlic in butter until dry.

Transfer to a large bowl and add cream cheese, sour cream, Tabasco, and garlic salt.

Stir to dip consistency.

Serve warm or at room temperature with toast points.

Makes 8 to 10 servings

Kitchen Note

- You can serve the marvelous dip immediately, or cover and refrigerate for up to 2 days.

Susan's Luscious Lemony Salad

My friend Susan Hill created this recipe after having a similar salad in Hawaii. She says, "This is a simple, crispy, clean salad, perfect with any meal! For nostalgia, I sprinkle it with toasted macadamia nuts."

3 tablespoons lemon juice

½ teaspoon salt

½ teaspoon sugar

⅓ cup canola oil or other vegetable oil

3 heads Bibb lettuce, washed, drained, and chilled

Black pepper

Sea salt, best available

Whisk together lemon juice, salt, and sugar in a small bowl. Add oil slowly, whisking until well blended.

Tear chilled Bibb lettuce into bite-size pieces into a large bowl.

Drizzle dressing over the lettuce and toss, coating well.

Grind black pepper over the top and sprinkle lightly with sea salt. Serve immediately.

Makes 8 servings

Oven-Roasted Tomatoes

Slow-roasting the tomatoes develops a deep, rich flavor. The balsamic vinegar adds a warm tang, and the garlic and fresh basil round out the flavors.

2 cups cherry tomatoes

1 large yellow and 1 large red tomato, cut into good-size wedges

6 large Roma tomatoes, quartered

3 tablespoons extra-virgin olive oil

2 tablespoons balsamic vinegar

6 large cloves garlic, peeled

½ teaspoon sugar

½ teaspoon salt

¼ teaspoon white pepper

8 large basil leaves, cut into chiffonade (see Kitchen Notes, page 76)

1 cup fresh or dried bread crumbs

Preheat the oven to 350°F. Grease a 9- by 13-inch baking dish.

In a large bowl, combine tomatoes, olive oil, vinegar, garlic, sugar, salt, and pepper; toss gently to combine.

Transfer to the prepared baking dish. Roast for 45 to 55 minutes, or until tomatoes have released their juices and are very fragrant.

Stir half of the basil into tomatoes and top with bread crumbs.

Return to the oven and roast for 15 to 20 minutes longer, or until bread crumbs are lightly toasted. Sprinkle with remaining basil and serve hot or at room temperature.

Makes 8 servings

Kitchen Note

- You may use any variety of tomatoes; sometimes yellow tomatoes are hard to find, so just use more of the red.

Shrimp and Eggplant Casserole

3 large eggplants, peeled, sliced, and seeded

1 cup chopped celery

1 onion, chopped

½ cup chopped fresh parsley

3 cloves garlic, crushed

8 tablespoons unsalted butter

2 pounds shrimp, peeled and deveined (see Kitchen Notes, below)

1 pound lump crabmeat, picked through to remove any pieces of shell

Beau Monde seasoning

Salt and black pepper

½ cup cooking sherry

1 cup + 2 tablespoons Italian dried bread crumbs

Preheat the oven to 350°F. Bring a large pot of salted water to a boil.

Boil eggplant in salted water until tender, 10 to 15 minutes. Drain and mash.

In a large skillet, sauté celery, onion, parsley, and garlic in 6 tablespoons of the butter until tender.

Add shrimp and cook until pink. Fold in crabmeat and cook until just heated through.

Stir in eggplant and season with Beau Monde seasoning, salt, and pepper to taste. Stir in sherry and 1 cup of the bread crumbs.

Scrape mixture into a 3-quart casserole and sprinkle top with remaining 2 tablespoons bread crumbs. Dot with remaining 2 tablespoons butter.

Bake for 20 to 25 minutes, or until heated through.

Makes 8 servings

Kitchen Notes

- I like to use extra-large shrimp (16 to 20 per pound) in this recipe.
- If you can't find Beau Monde seasoning, add some celery seed instead.

Shrimp and Eggplant Casserole (opposite),
Oven Roasted Tomatoes (page 109) and
Broccoli with Garlic and Pistachios (page 112)

Broccoli with Garlic and Pistachios

2 pounds broccoli

4 tablespoons extra-virgin olive oil

½ cup thinly sliced onion

3 cloves garlic, thinly sliced

¾ cup chicken broth

2 tablespoons unsalted butter

¼ teaspoon salt

½ cup shelled pistachios

Trim broccoli about 2 inches below florets and discard stems.

Heat 2 tablespoons of the olive oil in a 5- to 6-quart Dutch oven over medium heat. Add onion and garlic and sauté until tender, about 7 minutes.

Add broccoli and cook, tossing, for 1 minute.

Add chicken broth, butter, and salt. Bring to a boil and reduce the heat. Cover and simmer until broccoli is crisp-tender, 6 to 8 minutes.

Meanwhile, in a small skillet, sauté pistachios in remaining 2 tablespoons olive oil for 2 minutes.

Drain broccoli and transfer to a serving bowl. Sprinkle with pistachios and serve.

Makes 8 servings

Kitchen Note

● To easily slice garlic, cut each clove in half, placing the cut side down. Then slice thinly.

Rosemary Biscuits

2 cups all-purpose flour

1 tablespoon baking powder

¼ teaspoon baking soda

1 teaspoon salt

6 tablespoons vegetable shortening

1 cup buttermilk

¾ teaspoon crushed dried rosemary, or 2 teaspoons fresh rosemary, finely chopped

Sift flour, baking powder, baking soda, and salt together into a roomy bowl.

Cut in shortening with a pastry blender or a fork until the mixture is the texture of coarse meal.

Add buttermilk and mix lightly but thoroughly with your hands. Add a little more flour if dough is too sticky.

Knead for 1 minute. Work rosemary into dough.

Wrap dough in wax paper or foil and refrigerate until well chilled, at least 20 minutes.

Preheat the oven to 450°F.

Roll dough out ½ inch thick on a lightly floured surface or pastry cloth. (Always roll from center out for tender, crisp biscuits. See also Kitchen Notes, page 18).

Cut out rounds with a 2- or 2½-inch cutter.

Place rounds on a baking sheet. Bake for 10 to 12 minutes, or until golden brown.

Makes 12 biscuits

Super-Moist Carrot Cake
with Cream Cheese Frosting

"This classic carrot cake is one of our favorites. It's a great cake to make year-round or for a special occasion."

–Sara Foster

4 cups peeled and grated carrots

1½ cups coarsely chopped walnuts

1 cup dark raisins

2 cups all-purpose flour

1 tablespoon ground cinnamon

1 teaspoon ground cloves

2 teaspoons baking powder

1 teaspoon baking soda

1 teaspoon salt

4 large eggs

1 cup canola or safflower oil

1 cup granulated sugar

1 cup firmly packed light brown sugar

1 tablespoon pure vanilla extract

1 recipe Cream Cheese Frosting (recipe follows)

Preheat the oven to 350°F.

Grease and lightly flour two 9-inch cake pans and set aside.

Mix the carrots, walnuts, and raisins in a bowl and set aside.

Sift together the flour, cinnamon, cloves, baking powder, baking soda, and salt in a separate bowl and stir to mix; set aside.

Combine the eggs, oil, granulated sugar, brown sugar, and vanilla together in a separate bowl and whisk until well blended.

Slowly fold the flour mixture into the egg mixture and stir to blend just until all the dry ingredients are moist and blended. Do not overmix. Fold in the carrot mixture and stir just until combined.

Divide the batter evenly between the 2 prepared pans and bake 45 to 50 minutes, until the cakes are firm to the touch and a toothpick inserted in the center of each cake comes out clean.

Remove from the oven and cool the cakes 10 to 15 minutes in the pans. Remove from the pans and continue to cool on a baking rack.

Once the cakes have cooled completely, use a long, serrated knife to slice off the top rounded portion of each cake to make a flat, even surface. Discard the trimmings.

Place one of the layers cut side down on a cake plate. Top with about one-third of the frosting and spread evenly to cover the top of the cake layer. Place the next layer, cut side down, on top of the frosting and spread the top of the cake with about one-half of the remaining frosting. Use the remaining frosting to cover the sides of the cake.

Slice into portions and serve immediately or refrigerate until ready to serve. This cake keeps well for several days.

Makes one 9-inch layer cake; serves 10 to 12

Cream Cheese Frosting

½ pound (2 sticks) unsalted butter, softened

Two 8-ounce packages cream cheese, softened

5 cups confectioners' sugar

2 tablespoons grated orange zest or lemon zest

1 teaspoon pure vanilla extract

Place the butter and cream cheese in a bowl and cream together with an electric mixer until light and smooth.

Add the confectioners' sugar, 1 cup at a time, beating well after each addition until smooth.

Add the orange zest and vanilla and continue to mix lightly on high speed about 1 minute to make the frosting light and fluffy.

Makes about 3 cups frosting

Variations

Blackberry Cream Cheese Frosting: Fold in 1 cup fresh blackberries, which will swirl a bit of color into the frosting.

Coconut Cream Cheese Frosting: Add 2 cups sweetened flaked coconut and stir until well blended.

CHAPTER 11

My Favorite Tea Party

for 8 guests

If I had to choose a last meal, it would be a tea party. I firmly believe that the stresses and strains of modern life would be dramatically eased if we instituted the custom and ritual of afternoon tea. Fragrant tea served in a delicate china cup, a smattering of tiny finger sandwiches and bite-size sweets, and a chat with a good friend make life infinitely more pleasurable.

My first teatime experience was as a sophomore in college when I spent a semester studying in London. Afternoon tea, my friends and I quickly discovered, was the ticket to visiting the "nice" places we couldn't otherwise afford. We spent many an afternoon in the formal tearooms of London's finest hotels, partaking of dainty sweets and finger sandwiches, sipping exotic teas, laughing, and learning the customs of the remarkable country we had come to study.

Hosting afternoon tea parties came to be a favorite pastime of mine on this side of the Atlantic, too, and soon I began collecting the odd cup and saucer or teaspoon in antique shops and flea markets. As a young mother living in California, I introduced teatime to my toddler and his friends. My son, Martin, attended a Montessori school, where small children were taught how to handle "nice things." Likewise, we as parents were taught that children appreciate "real" things and shouldn't be relegated to plastic and paper utensils. To test the Montessori theory, I started using good dishes instead of paper products with my son and was pleased and surprised when they didn't go flying across the kitchen. The experience made a profound impression and taught me to have more confidence in the kids. Today, the most important thing I teach in my cooking classes is self-assurance in the kitchen, for both children and parents, and to not be afraid to try something different or to jump in and help.

When Martin turned 4, he and I began accompanying my friend Annette and her daughter, Madison, to tea at the Hotel Bel-Air in Beverly Hills. We enjoyed the enchanting atmosphere and the elegant selection of teas and foods, and the kids enthusiastically sampled anything that was offered. The memory of those magical afternoon tea parties will be with Martin and me forever.

Having a tea party gives me an excuse to get out all my pretty things, from linens to china. My mom and I share a love of tea sets and we have collected many a teapot and cup and saucer over the years. Cups don't just hold tea; they hold memories . . . and in our home, no teacups are more precious than the ones we salvaged from the rubble of our century-old family home on the Mississippi Gulf Coast after Hurricane Katrina. I have demitasse cups and saucers from my travels and from my grandmother, great-grandmother, and other dear people who have passed through my life (you'll see photos of some of them on the chapter introductions throughout the book).

I was delighted when my tea-party menu was chosen for the cover of this book. I called Mom to share the good news and her first words were, "I wish they had our tea sets." We picked out our favorite things and carefully packed them for the journey to the faraway city where the photography would be done. On the cover (in the background) you'll see the sterling-silver tea service that now resides in my living room and was given to me by my mother and to my mother by her father. The cups and plates are among those we salvaged, and the teaspoons are a gift to my mom from her friend Martha Stewart. And like the savvy entertainer she is, my mom even packed a box of sugar cubes, which she says are a must for any tea party.

Helping Hands

From the Seasoned Cook

Lady Bettye's delicious wafers have been handed down through many generations and require basic pastry skills. While you've got your experts in the baking mode, go ahead and have them help make the Plum Butter Cookies and Chocolate Chip Scones.

From the Kids

Kids can wash and dry the strawberries, then dip them. Let them make the thumbprints in the Plum Butter Cookies, fill with jam, and top with a pecan.

Smoked Salmon Pinwheels

1 (5-ounce) package Boursin cheese, softened

1 (3-ounce) package cream cheese, softened

1 (10-inch) sun-dried tomato tortilla

1 (10-inch) spinach tortilla

1 (10-inch) flour tortilla

8 ounces thinly sliced smoked salmon

Mix Boursin cheese and cream cheese in a medium bowl until combined.

Evenly spread cheese mixture on each tortilla, leaving a 1-inch border.

Layer smoked salmon evenly on top of cheese.

Roll up tortillas jelly-roll style and wrap tightly in plastic wrap. Refrigerate for 2 hours.

To serve, slice ½ inch from each end of roll. Cut remainder into 1-inch-wide pinwheels.

Makes 2 dozen pinwheels

Cucumber-Mint Tea Sandwiches

1 English cucumber, peeled and thinly sliced

Salt and white pepper

Dash white balsamic vinegar

16 thin slices white bread

8 ounces whipped cream cheese

16 fresh mint leaves

Sprinkle cucumber slices with salt, pepper, and vinegar. Drain on paper towels for 10 minutes. Pat dry.

Cut out a round from each piece of bread with a 2-inch cutter. Spread cream cheese on one side of each round.

Layer cucumber slices on top of the cream cheese. Add a tiny dab of cream cheese on top of the cucumber and top with a mint leaf.

Serve immediately or refrigerate, wrapped in plastic, until ready to serve, or up to 3 hours. If refrigerating, add mint leaves just before serving.

Makes 16 sandwiches

Kitchen Note

- For a variation, top the bread with sliced Roma tomatoes and a fresh basil leaf.

Egg Salad on Corn Muffins

⅓ cup mayonnaise, preferably homemade

1 tablespoon Dijon mustard

8 hard-boiled eggs, peeled and chopped

1 stalk celery, chopped

1 tablespoon chopped fresh dill

1 teaspoon MSG (optional)

12 regular corn muffins or 24 mini corn muffins (below)

Whisk mayonnaise and mustard together in a medium bowl. Add eggs, celery, dill, and MSG (if using), stir to blend.

Split corn muffins horizontally. Divide egg salad among the bottom halves of muffins, then top with the top halves and press together gently.

Serve immediately or wrap in plastic wrap and refrigerate until ready to serve, up to 3 hours.

Makes 12 or 24 sandwiches

Corn Muffins

½ cup white cornmeal

½ cup all-purpose flour

1 teaspoon baking powder

½ teaspoon salt

¼ teaspoon baking soda

1 large egg, beaten

1 cup buttermilk

Preheat the oven to 425°F. Grease a 12-cup muffin pan or 2 (12-cup) mini muffin pans generously with butter (or with a teaspoon of bacon fat in each cup, if you have it). Place pan in the preheating oven to melt the butter or bacon fat.

Combine cornmeal, flour, baking powder, salt, and baking soda in a large bowl.

Combine egg and buttermilk in a medium bowl; lightly mix into dry ingredients.

Carefully pour batter into the muffin cups, dividing equally. Return pan to oven and bake for 15 to 20 minutes for regular muffins or 10 to 12 minutes for mini muffins, or until the muffins are lightly browned.

Let cool and serve with Egg Salad (above), or serve hot, sliced, and buttered, if you like.

Makes 12 regular or 24 mini muffins

Egg Salad on Corn Muffins (opposite), Smoked Salmon
Pinwheels (page 119), and Cucumber-Mint Tea Sandwiches (page 119)

Paula's Mozzarella-Tomato Tart

No one knows mozzarella better than cheesemaker Paula Lambert, founder of the Mozzarella Company in Dallas, Texas. For over 20 years, her award-winning cheeses have found their way into the finest restaurants in America. "Fresh" is the key ingredient in her tart recipe, which boasts fresh tomatoes, fresh basil, and fresh mozzarella for a fantastic combination of flavors.

3 or 4 very ripe large tomatoes, cored and cut into ¼-inch-thick slices

Salt

1 sheet ready-to-bake puff pastry, thawed, at room temperature

1 large egg, lightly beaten

8 ounces fresh mozzarella cheese, cut into thin slices

Black pepper

2 stems (about 12 leaves) fresh basil leaves, cut into chiffonade (see Kitchen Notes, page 76)

Preheat the oven to 400°F. Butter an 11-inch tart pan with a removable bottom.

Line a rimmed baking sheet with paper towels. Place one layer of tomato slices on the paper towels, sprinkle lightly with salt, spread additional paper towels on the slices, and continue stacking and lightly salting the tomatoes. Cover the top tomatoes with paper towels and press down so that the tomatoes release their juices. Set aside for at least 30 minutes.

Place two pieces of plastic wrap next to each other on a flat surface and sprinkle with flour. Place puff pastry on top of one and sprinkle with flour. Place the second sheet of plastic wrap on top. Using a rolling pin, roll the dough out to a 12-inch circle.

Remove the top piece of plastic wrap. Invert the dough and center it in the prepared tart pan. With the plastic wrap still attached to the dough, use your fingers to press the dough to fit the pan. When the dough is well fitted, peel off the plastic wrap.

Roll the rolling pin over the edge of the tart pan to cut off the excess dough. Patch any holes with pieces from the cutoff dough.

Using a pastry brush, paint the bottom and sides of the pastry tart shell with the beaten egg. Bake the tart shell for 5 minutes.

Remove tart from the oven and distribute mozzarella over the crust. Arrange drained tomato slices in concentric circles on top of the cheese, overlapping them as if a spreading out a deck of cards. Grind black pepper over the tomatoes.

Return the tart to the oven and bake for 20 minutes, or until the cheese is completely melted and just beginning to brown and bubble and the tomatoes begin to brown slightly on their edges.

Sprinkle fresh basil over the tart. Slip off the outer ring of the tart pan. Using a long, flexible knife, separate the crust from the bottom and slide the tart onto a large serving plate.

Slice into wedges and serve while still warm.

Makes 8 servings

Lady Bettye's Cheese Wafers

This recipe was given to me by my friend Lady Bettye Nicholson. It is from the kitchen of Louise Dorsey Nicholson, her mother-in-law, who is now deceased.

10 ounces New York State sharp Cheddar cheese

1 cup margarine

2 cups all-purpose flour, plus more for dusting

Salt

Cayenne pepper

Grate cheese and blend with margarine in a mixer.

Add flour, a bit at a time. (Next comes the difficult part.)

When dough is blended, form into a ball and dust with flour. Wrap in wax paper and refrigerate for at least 30 minutes.

Preheat the oven to 350°F.

Pull off generous teaspoon-size portions of dough and roll them into thin rounds between two pieces of wax paper dusted with flour. Repeat with remaining dough. (Sometimes Bettye puts the rolled-out dough in the freezer in order to be able to better handle the rounds.)

Place the rounds on baking sheets. Sprinkle lightly with salt and cayenne. Bake for 5 to 10 minutes, or until lightly browned. Watch carefully—the wafers will brown very quickly.

Makes about 12 dozen wafers

Creamy Dreamy Trifle

1 (10-ounce) container whipped topping

½ cup sour cream

2 tablespoons sugar

½ teaspoon vanilla extract (optional)

2 cups fresh blueberries, rinsed

2 cups fresh raspberries, rinsed

2 tablespoons seedless raspberry jam

¼ pound prepared pound cake, cut into ½- to 1-inch pieces

Extra berries, cookies, toasted sliced almonds, and/or fresh mint leaves for garnish

In a medium bowl, combine whipped topping, sour cream, sugar, and vanilla (if using). Whisk until blended. Set aside.

Place blueberries in one medium bowl and raspberries in another. Gently stir 1 tablespoon of the jam and 1 teaspoon water into raspberries, and the remaining 1 tablespoon jam and 1 teaspoon water into blueberries until all fruit is coated.

Spoon ¼ cup of the raspberries or blueberries into the bottom of a tall, narrow (6- to 8-ounce) glass. Top with ¼ cup of the pound cake cubes, ¼ cup of the whipped topping mixture, ¼ cup of the berries, then another ¼ cup of the topping.

Garnish with berries, cookies, toasted sliced almonds, and/or mint.

Repeat with the remaining ingredients to make 8 trifles.

Makes 8 servings

Kitchen Note

- For tea-size servings, follow assembly instructions using stemmed sherry glasses and reduce each serving amount by one-half.

Creamy Dreamy Trifle (opposite)
and Chocolate Chip Scones with
Two Creams (page 126)

Chocolate Chip Scones
with Two Creams

Serve these delicious scones with both raspberry cream and my version of clotted cream. In an English high tea, clotted cream is traditionally used instead of butter, with jam spread on top of the cream. Bring out your favorite jams, if you like. You'll need to make the clotted cream at least 4 hours in advance of your party.

Clotted Cream

1 cup heavy cream, at room temperature

⅓ cup sour cream, at room temperature

1 tablespoon confectioners' sugar

Scones

2 cups all-purpose flour

⅔ cup + 2 teaspoons granulated sugar

1 teaspoon baking powder

½ teaspoon baking soda

6 tablespoons unsalted butter, chilled and diced

¾ cup milk chocolate chips

¾ cup milk

1 large egg yolk

1 teaspoon vanilla extract

2 tablespoons heavy cream

Raspberry Cream

1 cup heavy cream

¼ cup confectioners' sugar

½ cup raspberry preserves

Whole raspberries and mint leaves for garnish (optional)

To make clotted cream: In a medium bowl, with an electric mixer at medium speed, whip heavy cream until soft peaks form. Add sour cream and confectioners' sugar and beat until the mixture is thick. Refrigerate, covered, for at least 4 hours before using.

To make scones: Preheat the oven to 325°F. Line a large baking sheet with parchment paper.

In a large bowl, combine flour, ⅔ cup of granulated sugar, baking powder, and baking soda. Mix well.

Using a pastry blender, cut in butter until crumbly. Mix in chocolate chips.

In a medium bowl, whisk milk, egg yolk, and vanilla. Add to flour mixture and mix until dough comes together in moist clumps. Gather dough into a ball.

On a lightly floured surface, roll out dough to a 1-inch thickness.

Using a 2½-inch round cutter, cut scones and place on prepared baking sheet. Brush tops evenly with cream and sprinkle with remaining 2 teaspoons granulated sugar.

Bake for 20 minutes, or until lightly browned.

To make raspberry cream: In a medium bowl, with an electric mixer at medium speed, beat cream and confectioners' sugar until medium-soft peaks form.

Transfer to a serving bowl and fold in raspberry preserves until well combined. Garnish with fresh whole raspberries and mint leaves, if desired.

Serve warm scones with raspberry cream and/or clotted cream.

Makes 2 dozen scones

Strawberry Sparklers

12 ounces white chocolate bark

3 dozen strawberries

Red, green, or blue sugar; or edible hot pink glitter (see Kitchen Note, below)

Place chocolate in a microwavable bowl and melt in a microwave oven according to package directions.

Place strawberries in a large bowl (make sure the bowl and strawberries are dry; even a little moisture will alter the texture of chocolate when strawberries are dipped).

One by one, dip strawberries halfway into melted chocolate and then one quarter of the way into red sugar or edible glitter.

Makes 3 dozen sparklers

Kitchen Note

- Instead of the red sugar or edible glitter, decorate with red or pink "icing." Place coated strawberries on wax paper. While the chocolate hardens, mix 3 tablespoons of melted white chocolate with a few drops of red food coloring, until desired shade of pink or red is reached. Place this "icing" into a piping bag and pipe decorations on the strawberries. (If you don't have a piping bag, use a zip-top bag: Spoon icing into the corner of the bag and seal. Cut a very small opening at the corner and squeeze out the icing.)

Plum Butter Cookies

1½ cups unsalted butter, at room temperature

1 cup sugar

1 large egg yolk

1 large egg

2 teaspoons vanilla extract

3 cups all-purpose flour

⅛ teaspoon salt

⅓ cup plum preserves

1 cup pecan halves

Preheat the oven to 325°F. Line a baking sheet with parchment paper.

Cream butter and sugar until smooth.

Add egg yolk, egg, and vanilla and beat until fluffy.

Beat in flour and salt. Be careful not to overbeat.

Shape 1 teaspoon of dough into a ball and place on prepared baking sheet. Make a small indentation on the top with your thumb and fill with ¼ teaspoon preserves. Top with a pecan half. Repeat with remaining dough, preserves, and pecans.

Bake cookies for 10 to 12 minutes, or until bottoms just begin to brown.

Makes 4 dozen cookies

Kitchen Note

- For a variation, use your favorite preserves or jam.

Coconut Lemon Tartlets

The Best Pie Crust (page 194) or store-bought unbaked pie crust

½ cup pecans, chopped

3 large eggs, beaten

1½ cups sugar

½ teaspoon lemon zest

4 teaspoons lemon juice

1 teaspoon vanilla extract

½ cup unsalted butter, melted

1¼ cups sweetened, flaked coconut

Preheat the oven to 350°F. Grease a 12-cup mini muffin pan.

Cut pie pastry into rounds with a 2-inch cutter.

Press rounds into cups of the muffin pan. Sprinkle pecans evenly into each cup.

Combine eggs, sugar, lemon zest, lemon juice, and vanilla in a medium bowl and beat well.

Stir in melted butter. Fold in coconut.

Fill each muffin cup two-thirds full with batter.

Bake for 20 minutes, or until golden brown.

Makes 1 dozen tartlets

Kitchen Note

● You can use premade frozen pie dough as a speedy shortcut, leaving only the filling to make.

CHAPTER 12

Something's on the Grill

for 8 guests

My brother Richard is the grilling expert in the family. He usually cooks on the grill four or five nights a week, and with four kids and a handful of grandkids there are always lots of mouths to feed. His skill at the grill is well known among family, friends, and colleagues—a meal cooked by Richard is a much anticipated treat. Using the grill as a tool to cook most anything, Richard's grilling repertoire is limited only by his imagination. He moves beyond the requisite steaks and burgers to wild game, quail, chicken, seafood, vegetables, and desserts. In this chapter, I share his recipes for beef tenderloin and pork tenderloin (use whichever you prefer), as well as grilled vegetables. Grilling brings out the flavor in most any vegetable, so don't limit yourself to asparagus. Use what is on hand and in season and always bring the vegetables to room temperature before placing on the grill. Use a grill topper or grill basket to keep thinner vegetables from falling through.

While Richard works his magic on the grill, his wife, Mary, bakes a creamy dish of layered potatoes and cheese in the oven. For Grilled Corn Salsa, I prep everything ahead of time. The corn is the first thing on the grill and the last thing to go into the salsa. Hot Artichoke Parmesan Dip is a classic quick-and-easy dish that my mom gave me when I first started entertaining. It's perfect before the meal while everyone is hanging around the grill or visiting in the kitchen.

A salad of grilled peaches is a refreshing and tasty alternative to greens and a rare treat in late summer when peaches are at their peak.

When looking for a dessert for the grill, where else to look but the legendary Viking Cooking School, whose teachers are all authorities on grilling. Grilled Pound Cake is the perfect dessert for a grill menu. You can make or buy the cake, and ice cream and rum sauce make it doubly delicious.

A few years ago, my mom and I catered a housewarming party for my youngest brother and his wife. We planned a delicious menu and turned to Richard and his grill for the main course—Beef Tenderloin on sourdough rolls with an assortment of sauces. Delicious alone or with rolls and sauces, I can honestly say that it's the best I've ever had.

Helping Hands

Help from the Seasoned Cook

An experienced grill cook is required to season the tenderloin and oversee the grilling. The asparagus and peaches can be grilled while the meat rests and can go from the grill directly to the plate (top the peaches with cheese at the last minute).

Help from the Kids

Snapping the asparagus at their natural break, shucking corn, and brushing the pound cake with butter are helpful and kid-friendly tasks.

Hot Artichoke Parmesan Dip

1 (14-ounce) can artichoke hearts, drained

1¼ cups grated Parmesan cheese

1 cup mayonnaise

1 teaspoon lemon juice

⅛ teaspoon garlic salt

Dash Worcestershire sauce

Unsalted wafers or crackers, for serving

Preheat the oven to 350°F.

In a mixing bowl, mash together artichoke hearts, 1 cup of the Parmesan, the mayonnaise, lemon juice, garlic salt, and Worcestershire.

Transfer to a small ovenproof dish and cover with remaining ¼ cup Parmesan.

Bake for about 10 minutes, or until dip is warm throughout and cheese is melted. Serve with wafers.

Makes 8 servings

Fresh Market Peaches with Blue Cheese

1 cup crumbled blue cheese, at room temperature

1 teaspoon extra-virgin olive oil, plus more for brushing

4 peaches, peeled and halved (don't blanch before peeling)

3 tablespoons pine nuts, toasted (see page 170)

Heat a barbecue grill to medium-high.

In a small bowl, mash together blue cheese and olive oil with a fork. Cover and refrigerate until ready to use.

Brush peach halves with olive oil. Place cut side down on grill and grill until heated through, 3 to 5 minutes.

Top each peach half with about 2 tablespoons cheese and sprinkle with toasted pine nuts.

Makes 8 servings

Richard's Beef Tenderloin

5- or 6-pound beef tenderloin

Olive oil

Powdered Worcestershire

Kosher salt and coarsely ground black pepper

Trim tenderloin of any visible fat and place in a glass dish. Rub liberally with olive oil and sprinkle with Worcestershire. Cover and refrigerate for 4 hours.

Bring tenderloin to room temperature.

Heat a barbecue grill to high.

Sprinkle tenderloin with salt and pepper. Place on grill over direct heat and sear on all sides.

Move from directly over flame and grill for 20 to 25 minutes, or until medium-rare (135°F) in the center and more done at the ends.

Let stand 10 minutes before cutting.

Makes 8 to 10 servings

Kitchen Note

- You can find powdered Worcestershire in the spice section of most good supermarkets.

Grilled Asparagus

While the beef or pork tenderloin is standing, grill the asparagus.

2 pounds asparagus, trimmed

Olive oil

Salt and coarsely ground black pepper

Heat a barbecue grill to medium-high.

Lightly coat asparagus with olive oil. Sprinkle with salt and pepper.

Grill asparagus, turning, until crisp-tender, about 5 minutes.

Makes 8 servings

Kitchen Note

- Red peppers from the grill go well with the asparagus.

Richard's Beef Tenderloin (opposite),
Fresh Market Peaches with Blue Cheese (page 133), and Grilled Asparagus (opposite)

Richard's Pork Tenderloin

3- to 4-pound pork tenderloin

Olive oil

½ cup Allegro Original Marinade

½ cup Worcestershire sauce

½ cup red wine vinegar

Salt and black pepper

Creole seasoning

Coat tenderloin liberally with olive oil and place in a glass dish.

Combine marinade, Worcestershire, and vinegar and pour over tenderloin. Cover and refrigerate for up to half a day.

Bring tenderloin to room temperature.

Heat barbecue grill to high. Preheat the oven to 400°F.

Remove tenderloin from marinade and sprinkle with salt, pepper, and Creole seasoning. Reserve marinade.

Place pork tenderloin on hot grill over direct heat and sear on all sides. Move from directly over flame and grill for 10 to 15 minutes or longer, to desired doneness. (Pork is so lean these days, be sure not to overcook or it will be dry.) Let stand 10 minutes before slicing.

While pork is standing, bring reserved marinade to a boil in a small saucepan. Boil briefly, then remove from the heat. Cut tenderloin into 1½-inch-thick slices. Place meat slices and marinade in a baking dish.

Bake for 8 minutes, basting with the marinade halfway through cooking. Serve immediately.

Makes 8 to 10 servings

Grilled Corn Salsa

4 ears fresh corn, on the cob

About 5 tablespoons extra-virgin olive oil

½ medium red onion, cut into ¼-inch dice

2 ripe plum tomatoes, seeded and cut into ¼-inch dice

½ ripe avocado, cut into ¼-inch dice

2 tablespoons fresh lemon juice

1 tablespoon chopped fresh parsley

1 teaspoon finely chopped jalapeño chile pepper

½ teaspoon finely minced garlic

Salt and black pepper

Heat a barbecue grill to high.

Remove husks and silk from each ear of corn. Brush ears with 2 to 4 tablespoons olive oil.

Grill corn, turning occasionally, until all sides are well grilled, about 10 minutes.

In a serving bowl, combine 1 tablespoon of the olive oil and the onion, tomatoes, avocado, lemon juice, parsley, jalapeño, and garlic.

Transfer corn to a plate and sprinkle with salt and pepper.

When corn is cool enough to handle, cut the kernels from the ears.

Stir corn into salsa. Cover and refrigerate for up to 1 day.

Serve at room temperature.

Makes 4 cups

Boursin New Potatoes

Butter for coating baking dish

2 cups whipping cream

5 ounces Boursin cheese

3 pounds medium red potatoes, thinly sliced

1 teaspoon salt

1 teaspoon black pepper

Chopped fresh parsley, for garnish

Preheat the oven to 400°F. Coat the bottom and sides of a 9- by 13-inch baking dish with butter.

Heat cream and cheese in a medium saucepan over medium heat, stirring frequently, until cheese is melted.

Arrange half of the sliced potatoes, slightly overlapping, in the prepared baking dish and sprinkle with salt and pepper. Top with half of the cheese sauce. Repeat with remaining potatoes and sauce.

Cover and bake for 30 minutes.

Uncover and bake for 30 minutes longer, or until the potatoes are tender. Sprinkle with parsley and serve.

Makes 8 servings

Grilled Pound Cake with Macadamia Ice Cream and Rum Caramel Sauce

Toasting pound cake on the grill makes it extra special. The deep rich flavor of caramel is a natural for partnering with sweet dark rum. (Make some without the rum for the kids.) The result is "grown-up" caramel sauce that's hard to resist. Serve the cake with the sauce—or with chocolate sauce, if you prefer.

Rum Caramel Sauce

- 1 cup sugar
- ½ cup water
- 1 cup heavy cream
- 2 teaspoons Myers's rum or other dark rum
- 4 tablespoons unsalted butter, cut into 4 to 6 pieces

Pound Cake

- Buttermilk Pound Cake (page 199) or 1 store-bought pound cake
- ½ cup unsalted butter, melted
- Macadamia Ice Cream (opposite)

To make caramel sauce: Combine sugar and water in a medium saucepan over medium heat. Slowly bring to a simmer, swirling to dissolve sugar, about 6 minutes.

Increase the heat to medium-high. Cover and cook for 2 minutes. Uncover and swirl the pan from time to time to distribute the heat evenly; *do not stir.* Cook until sugar is medium dark amber in color.

Carefully whisk in cream and rum. Do not panic if sauce begins to clump; just continue whisking constantly and vigorously until completely smooth, then whisk in butter.

Serve sauce warm or at room temperature.

To grill cake: Clean the barbecue grill grates with a stiff brush, then oil liberally to prevent sticking. Heat grill to medium. (If using a grill pan, lightly oil and preheat grill pan to medium-high heat.)

Cut pound cake into 8 slices. Brush slices on both sides with melted butter.

Grill pound cake slices until nicely toasted on both sides.

Place grilled pound cake onto a platter. Serve with scoops of Macadamia Ice Cream (opposite) and top with caramel sauce.

Makes 8 servings

Kitchen Note

- The sauce can be made up to 3 days in advance. Gently reheat before serving.

Macadamia Ice Cream

3 large egg yolks

¼ cup sugar

1 cup whole milk

1 cup heavy cream

1 teaspoon vanilla extract

¾ cup chopped toasted macadamia nuts

Whisk egg yolks and sugar together in a medium bowl until yolks are pale yellow in color.

In a small saucepan, bring milk just to the boiling point over medium heat.

Add a small amount of the hot milk to egg mixture and stir to combine. Stir in remaining milk, then pour mixture back into the pan and return to the heat.

Cook, stirring constantly with a wooden spoon, until mixture coats the back of the spoon.

Remove from heat. Strain through a fine mesh strainer into a clean mixing bowl. Place the bowl over an ice bath to cool.

When cool, stir in cream and vanilla; refrigerate until cold.

Place mixture in the bowl of an ice cream machine and freeze according to the manufacturer's directions.

When ice cream has reached a soft-serve consistency, mix in toasted macadamia nuts.

Transfer ice cream to a storage container. Press a piece of plastic wrap onto the surface, seal the container, and freeze until firm, about 3 hours.

Makes 8 servings

Kitchen Note

- To toast macadamia nuts in the oven, spread in a single layer on a baking sheet. Toast in a 350°F oven, shaking the pan occasionally, until light golden brown. To toast on the stove top, place the nuts in a dry sauté pan large enough to accommodate them in a single layer. Place over medium heat and cook, stirring frequently, until they begin to color. Remove from the heat, then immediately remove from the hot pan to stop the browning process.

CHAPTER 13

Shrimp Under the Oak Trees

for 8 guests

There are two ancient oak trees at 1215 East Beach in the little Gulf Coast town of Pass Christian, Mississippi. The big white two-story house set back from the Gulf of Mexico looks cool and peaceful with big screened porches on each side. The massive oak trees that frame the old house have enormous limbs, some reaching down toward the earth as if to offer an invitation to swing or climb on their sturdy limbs. The rustle of the Gulf breeze through the trees tells you that this is a very special place, a happy place where family and friends love to gather.

As you drive up the long driveway made of broken seashells you have an immediate feeling of peace and tranquillity—that is, until you drive around back and realize that's where the action is taking place. The swimming pool overflows with children and grandchildren; and under the big oak tree, my father waits impatiently for the water to boil to cook his shrimp in the butane cooker. The shrimp goes in first; then the corn and potatoes will boil in the shrimp- and spice-seasoned water. Back at the house my mother is relaxed in a white wicker chair on the screened porch entertaining the grown-ups.

Whether we had out-of-town guests or a house full of family, our meals always showcased the bounty of the Gulf. No matter who you are or where you were from, if you paid a summer visit to the Puckett family in Pass Christian, you are familiar with this meal.

The tablecloth consists of yesterday's newspaper, which can easily be rolled up and thrown out at the end of the messy meal. For napkins we use colorful dish towels in seashell napkin rings. To keep from constant dishwashing when the house is teeming with children and guests, another family tradition is to letter each person's name on a large plastic cup. This serves as a makeshift place card as well as one's personal cup for the day. Soft drinks are in washtubs and everyone selects his or her own.

When the shrimp is cooked, word goes out to our large, noisy family that supper is ready. The swimming pool empties and everyone heads to the house. While the children are getting dressed, the grown-ups gather in the kitchen to eat our favorite seafood dish, Ben's Bar-B-Q Shrimp (my Dad's recipe). It is ladled into individual bowls with the shrimp swimming in a delicious sauce. The po' boy bread is passed and all conversation stops. Regardless of what your mother taught you about dipping and sopping, all rules are suspended and we dip our bread in the spicy barbecue sauce. After the dishes have been removed, the rest of the group gathers. Big earthenware bowls of boiled shrimp (yes, more shrimp; we love it), potatoes, and corn are placed on the table. Sauces line the table in several bowls, so there is not much reaching, and butter is placed strategically up and down the table for corn. A large bowl of romaine lettuce salad with bright red cherry tomatoes, carrots, and a tangy dressing is passed. Some of the adults are called on to peel shrimp for the youngest of the group, but usually the art of shrimp-peeling is taught to Coast children at an early age.

When the bowls are empty and everyone begins to push their chairs back, we wipe our shrimp-stained hands. Then a basket of refreshing ice cream sandwiches appears. After the newspaper table covering has been rolled up and tossed out, we are still gathered around the table telling stories of past summers in this wonderful, magical house.

The ancient oak trees still stand at 1215 East Beach, but our beautiful century-old home is gone, a victim of Hurricane Katrina. Most of the historic town of Pass Christian is gone, too. Wind and water can destroy homes, but they can't erase memories. And the remembrance of shrimp cooked under the oak trees and my family and friends gathered at the kitchen table will be with me forever.

Helping Hands

Help from the Seasoned Cook

Ben's Bar-B-Q Shrimp and the boiled shrimp, corn, and new potatoes require a little more effort as seasonings are important to the success of the dishes.

Help from the Kids

Have the kids help make Teensy's Chocolate Chip Treats (page 28) and then they can assemble the ice cream sandwiches. Just remember to wrap immediately and freeze so the ice cream does not melt. Shucking the corn is another job where kids are a big help.

Ben's Bar-B-Q Shrimp
with Po' Boy Bread

1 (10-ounce) bottle Lea & Perrins Worcestershire sauce

1 (16-ounce) bottle Wishbone Italian dressing

Juice of 6 lemons

2 cups unsalted butter, melted

¼ cup lemon pepper

5 pounds extra-large shrimp, unpeeled

Po' boy or French bread

Mix Worcestershire, Italian dressing, lemon juice, butter, and lemon pepper in a medium bowl.

Pour mixture over shrimp in a large bowl. Cover and marinate shrimp in the refrigerator for at least 6 hours (overnight is good).

Preheat the oven to 350°F.

Transfer shrimp and sauce to a baking dish and cover. Bake for 25 to 30 minutes, or until shrimp is cooked through (check after 20 minutes).

Serve in a bowl, shells on, with bread for the sauce. Peel as you eat.

Makes 8 servings

Kitchen Notes

- The secret is not to cook the shrimp too long, or they will be hard to peel.
- We prefer extra-large shrimp, but large shrimp work fine.
- Check with your local fish market to see when the freshest seafood is available.

Boiled Shrimp, Corn, and New Potatoes

Spread out plenty of newspaper for this messy feast and serve with bowls of Spicy Seafood Sauce (page 146) and Tasty Tartar Sauce (page 146) and lots of butter for the corn.

1 (5-ounce) package crab boil	3 pounds new potatoes, scrubbed
5 pounds large shrimp	8 ears corn, shucked and broken in half

To boil shrimp: Fill a large pot with a basket insert about two-thirds with water and add crab boil. Bring to a rolling boil.

Place shrimp in the basket and lower into the water. Cook until shrimp are cooked through (test after 4 to 5 minutes, though shrimp may need a minute or more of additional cooking). Do not overcook.

Lift out the basket to drain water back into the pot. Pour shrimp over ice to keep them from cooking more.

To boil potatoes: Place potatoes in the basket, lower into the water, and cook for 12 to 15 minutes, or until cooked through.

Lift out the basket to drain the water back into the pot. Transfer potatoes to a large bowl; keep warm.

To boil corn: Place corn in the basket and lower into water. Try not to let corn sit at the bottom of the pot, as it will absorb too much of the hot spices.

Boil for 8 to 10 minutes, or until tender.

Serve shrimp, potatoes, and corn as soon as corn is done.

Makes 8 servings

Kitchen Notes

- For a successful shrimp boil, boiling the shrimp in an 8- to 10-quart pot with a basket insert over a butane burner outside is the very best! If this is not available, the same size pot does well on the stove.

- Refrigerate raw shrimp in bowls of ice or a cooler filled with ice until ready to cook.

- The best size shrimp for this recipe are large; they are easy to peel, and tender.

- For an appetizer: When you are at the fish market, pick up a quart of fresh oysters and serve with Spicy Seafood Sauce (page 146) and crackers.

Spicy Seafood Sauce

1 cup chili sauce

1 cup ketchup

2 tablespoons lemon juice

1½ tablespoons grated horseradish (optional)

1½ tablespoons Worcestershire sauce

8 dashes Tabasco sauce

Salt

Mix all of the ingredients in a medium bowl. Divide sauce among several smaller bowls for serving.

Makes about 2 cups

Kitchen Notes

- You can make the sauce 2 or 3 days ahead of time as it keeps well in the refrigerator.

- The sauce—ideal with Boiled Shrimp, Corn, and New Potatoes (page 144)—is also especially good with oysters as an appetizer.

- When serving this sauce with any kind of seafood, you'll probably want to also pass a bottle of Tabasco at the table so the diehards can kick up the heat.

Tasty Tartar Sauce

1 cup mayonnaise

3 tablespoons chopped pickle

2 tablespoons chopped stuffed olives

1 tablespoon chopped capers

1 tablespoon chopped fresh parsley

1 teaspoon chopped onion

Mix all ingredients in a medium bowl and chill. Divide sauce among several smaller bowls for serving.

Makes 1½ cups

Rivers's Romaine Salad with Homemade Garlic Croutons

If you have the time, make your own croutons for this salad. Either garlic or herbed croutons would go well here.

1 cup extra-virgin olive oil

½ cup balsamic vinegar

1½ teaspoons Grey Poupon Dijon mustard (made with white wine)

Pinch garlic salt

3 heads romaine lettuce, cleaned and torn

2 cups cherry tomatoes, halved

1 cup chopped carrots

1 cup grated Parmesan cheese

½ cup chopped fresh parsley

Homemade Garlic Croutons (below, optional)

Whisk together olive oil, vinegar, mustard, and garlic salt in a small bowl.

In a salad bowl, toss together lettuce, tomatoes, carrots, Parmesan, and parsley.

When ready to serve, add enough dressing to salad to coat leaves and toss. Sprinkle with croutons.

Makes 8 servings

Garlic Croutons

⅔ cup olive oil (approximately)

4 thick slices day-old French or Italian bread, cut into ¾-inch cubes

2 large garlic cloves, halved

In a large skillet, heat oil over medium heat. Add bread cubes, turning each one to coat with oil. Cook until bread cubes are brown on all sides and are very crispy. (Add more oil, if necessary, for the bread to absorb as much oil as possible without becoming soggy.)

Remove from heat and let cool briefly. Rub each bread cube with garlic.

Makes 4 cups

Summer Fruit Cobbler

Substitute blueberries, apples, or raspberries for the peaches and blackberries, if you like. Serve the cobbler warm with a scoop of vanilla ice cream (if you're not already having the ice cream sandwiches (opposite). During the Christmas holidays, I substitute a cup of whole-cranberry relish for the berries, and apples for the peaches, and sprinkle the top with cinnamon sugar for a festive berry dessert.

Fruit

3 tablespoons unsalted butter

4 to 5 large peaches, peeled and cut into bite-size pieces

⅓ cup sugar

1 tablespoon fresh lemon juice

1 cup fresh blackberries

Topping

5 tablespoon unsalted butter

1 cup all purpose flour

⅔ cup sugar

1½ teaspoons baking powder

½ teaspoon salt

1 cup heavy cream

1 egg yolk

Vanilla ice cream (optional)

For the fruit: In a large skillet, heat butter over medium heat. Add peaches, sugar, and lemon juice. Cook until softened, 2 to 3 minutes.

Gently toss in blackberries and stir just to coat. Remove the pan from the heat and set aside.

For the topping: Preheat the oven to 350°F. Place butter in a 9-inch square baking pan and put in the oven to melt.

Meanwhile, combine flour, sugar, baking powder, and salt in a large bowl. Add cream and egg yolk and mix well.

Remove the baking pan from the oven and pour the butter into the batter, leaving just enough in the baking pan to coat it.

Spoon fruit mixture into the baking pan and pour batter on top.

Bake for 25 minutes. If the top is brown, cover loosely with foil and continue to bake for another 10 to 15 minutes, or until a toothpick inserted in the center comes out clean. Cool slightly before serving with ice cream, if desired.

Makes 8 servings

Homemade Brownie Ice Cream Sandwiches

Brownies

1½ sticks unsalted butter + 1 tablespoon (at room temperature) for greasing foil

¾ cup unsweetened cocoa powder

1½ cups sugar

3 large eggs

2 teaspoons vanilla extract

1½ cups all-purpose flour

Pinch of salt

Sandwiches

1 quart vanilla ice cream, softened

Rainbow or chocolate sprinkles

Chopped pecans

To make brownies: Preheat the oven to 350°F.

Line the bottom and sides of a 9- by 13-inch baking pan with aluminum foil, leaving ½ inch of foil extending from the edges. Lightly grease the foil with 1 tablespoon of the butter.

Melt remaining 1½ sticks butter in a large saucepan over medium heat. Remove the saucepan from the heat and whisk in cocoa powder until the mixture is smooth and no lumps remain. Add sugar and continue whisking until well blended. Let the mixture cool slightly. Add eggs and vanilla and mix until well blended. Add flour and salt and mix until well blended.

Pour the batter into the prepared baking pan and spread evenly.

Bake for 20 minutes, or until a toothpick inserted into the center of the brownie comes out clean. Let cool completely in the pan.

Use the foil to lift out the brownie onto a cutting board. Cut the brownie in half lengthwise. Carefully loosen both halves from the foil.

To make sandwiches: Cut a piece of foil large enough to enclose the two brownie halves when placed on top of one another. Place one half on the foil. Spread the softened ice cream evenly over the brownie in a layer about 1 inch thick. Top with the other half of the brownie and press down gently. Enclose in the foil. Freeze 4 to 6 hours, or until hard.

Peel away the foil and cut into 8 to 10 ice cream sandwiches.

Place sprinkles and pecans in separate flat dishes. Coat sides of ice cream sandwiches in either or both. Serve immediately.

Makes 8 to 10 ice cream sandwiches

CHAPTER 14

Sweetheart Dinner for Two

for 2 guests

O ften the best gatherings are gatherings of two. Turn off the phone and light the candles; an intimate "at home" dinner for two is the perfect remedy for a harried workweek when quality time with a loved one has been elusive. I know several couples who make a practice of scheduling sweetheart dinners, but none match the fun and flair of my friends John Currence and his beautiful wife, Bess. John, who learned to cook at the apron strings of his mother in New Orleans, is chef-owner of the widely acclaimed City Grocery in Oxford, Mississippi. It was his good fortune to lure Bess away from her life as a literary agent in New York City to a small town in the Deep South. Some say it was John's generous spirit and tenacious pursuit that won her heart, but I'm not alone in the opinion that his magnificent cooking had something to do with it, too. John and Bess love to have small dinner parties, where John does the cooking and Bess takes care of the preparation and cleanup. Their best dinners, however, are the ones they plan for each other. I asked John to create a candlelight dinner for two that evoked their honeymoon in France, and he's simplified the recipes so that Bess (who doesn't cook much) can handle them herself. (He's also generously sized the recipes, so you'll have delicious leftovers.)

So many of the great meals Bess and John have shared have started with a pâté, and this one is particularly simple. It's easy to prepare and uses basic ingredients, but guests will think you're a brilliant cook and have worked for hours. John's mother makes a pâté similar to this one every year at Christmas and it's become so coveted that her list of people who want it grows each year. As a result, the Currence household now spends about a week and a half each year making pâté.

Coq au Vin is a classic comfort food and works beautifully with Apple Cider Wilted Spinach and Herbed Rice Pilaf. John claims to be uncertain whether Bess loves him or this red wine–braised bird more. She swears it's the best thing she's ever eaten and he loves her for her simple and honest tastes.

On their honeymoon, the Currences spent a week on a barge traveling through the French countryside. Though the scenery was wonderful, the food on the boat was slightly less impressive. But, as is occasionally the case, the kitchen ended up with a mistake that became a wonderful invention. The chef made chocolate mousse for dessert, and as he was finishing it, he decided it was not quite chocolaty enough, so he added grated dark chocolate at the end. The chocolate, of course, didn't melt; but it did add a great new texture to the lighter mousse. John has stolen the chef's mistake and passed it on to you—the perfect ending for a Sweetheart Dinner for Two.

Helping Hands

Skip the Help from the Seasoned Cook and the Kids

Since this is a romantic meal for two, you won't be wanting extra help. The fun comes from preparing the meal with one special person. Start a day early since the chicken must marinate overnight. In addition, the mousse must sit for a couple of hours before it can be served. Of course, if you decide to make the meal for a bigger gang, bring in the helping hands. The kids will enjoy stemming the spinach.

Cognac-Scented Chicken Liver Pâté

2 tablespoons unsalted butter

3 tablespoons minced shallots

2 teaspoons chopped garlic

½ pound chicken livers

1½ tablespoons fresh thyme leaves

¾ teaspoon cayenne pepper

2 teaspoons salt

2 teaspoons fresh cracked black pepper

1¼ cups chopped button mushrooms

¾ cup cognac

¼ cup heavy cream

French bread, for serving

Melt butter in a large skillet over medium heat. Sauté shallots and garlic until transparent.

Stir in chicken livers, thyme, cayenne, salt, and black pepper and cook until livers are plump and firm to the touch.

Add mushrooms and cook until tender.

Stir in cognac and cook, stirring constantly, until there is almost no liquid remaining.

Stir in cream and combine well.

Blend mixture in a food processor until smooth.

Pack pâté into individual ramekins (or other little serving bowls) and allow to cool to room temperature.

Cover with plastic wrap and refrigerate until ready to serve.

Serve with freshly sliced French bread.

Makes 2 servings (with leftovers)

Kitchen Note

- This easy-to-make pâté can be prepared up to a week in advance and packed in serving containers, covered, and refrigerated.

Coq auj Vin (opposite), Apple Cider Wilted Spinach (page 156),
and Herbed Rice Pilaf (page 156)

Coq au Vin

3- to 4-pound whole chicken, rinsed and
patted dry

Salt and black pepper

14 sprigs fresh rosemary

6 cups Burgundy wine

6 strips bacon, chopped

12 small button or cremini mushrooms, sliced

1 large baking potato, cubed

1 medium yellow onion, chopped

2 large carrots, sliced

2 stalks celery, sliced

12 cloves garlic, coarsely chopped

10 sprigs fresh thyme

4 sprigs fresh sage

½ cup good-quality olive oil

4 cups low-sodium beef broth

Season inside and outside of chicken with salt and pepper. Stuff the cavity with 10 of the rosemary sprigs and place bird in a tall, narrow container. Add the Burgundy. Cover the container and marinate chicken in the refrigerator for 24 hours, turning chicken over a few times during that time.

Preheat the oven to 375°F. Drain chicken, reserving wine. Pat chicken dry with paper towels.

In a Dutch oven, cook bacon until just crisp. Transfer bacon to a bowl and set aside, leaving drippings in the pan.

Toss mushrooms, potato, onion, carrots, celery, garlic, thyme, sage, and remaining 4 sprigs rosemary in a large bowl with ¼ cup of the olive oil. Season with salt and pepper.

Add remaining ¼ cup olive oil to bacon drippings. Dump vegetables into the pan and brown lightly over medium heat. Transfer vegetables to a large bowl and set aside.

Add chicken to the pan and brown both top and bottom. Finish with bird sitting in the pan breast up. Return vegetables and cooked bacon to the pan and pour broth and reserved red wine over all. Cover and bake for 1 hour.

Uncover and bake, spooning wine over chicken every 5 minutes, for 45 minutes, or until chicken is cooked through and juices run clear when chicken is pierced with a knife.

Transfer chicken to a serving platter. Remove vegetables with a slotted spoon and place around chicken.

Place the pan over high heat and reduce the liquid to about 2 cups. Season with salt and pepper.

Pour sauce over the chicken and vegetables and serve. (You can cut up chicken before presenting it, but the whole chicken surrounded by the vegetables looks beautiful.)

Makes 2 servings (with leftovers)

Apple Cider Wilted Spinach

1 tablespoon unsalted butter

6 cups spinach, stemmed

Salt and white pepper

3 tablespoons apple cider vinegar

Melt butter in a large skillet over medium heat. Add spinach and immediately turn with tongs, seasoning lightly with salt and white pepper.

Drizzle in vinegar and continue turning until spinach is wilted completely.

Makes 2 servings

Herbed Rice Pilaf

1½ tablespoons unsalted butter

½ cup chopped yellow onion

2 teaspoons chopped garlic

1½ cups white rice

½ cup white wine

1 teaspoon dried thyme

1½ teaspoons salt

1½ teaspoons white pepper

2½ cups chicken broth

Preheat the oven to 375°F.

Melt butter in a medium saucepan over medium heat. Stir in onion and garlic and sauté until transparent. Add rice and stir until coated with butter. Stir in wine and thyme and coat rice again. Add salt and pepper. Stir in chicken broth. Cover and bake for 20 minutes, or until rice is just tender. If any liquid remains, return the pan to the oven (uncovered) for a couple of minutes, or until rice absorbs liquid.

Makes 2 servings (with leftovers)

Kitchen Note

- A great rule of thumb for perfectly cooked rice is this: Before pouring the broth over the rice, smooth the rice out flat in the pan. Then add just enough broth to come as high as the first joint of your index finger while the tip is touching the top of the rice. I learned this from a Cajun cook on a tugboat I was working on in the Gulf of Mexico in 1983, and it is how I have cooked rice for 25 years. Whether I'm cooking for 5 or 500, it never fails.

Two-Chocolate Mousse "Mistake"

½ pound milk chocolate, chopped

¼ cup strong coffee

6 tablespoons unsalted butter, softened

3 large eggs, separated

3 tablespoons Chambord (raspberry liqueur)

1 cup heavy cream

4 tablespoons confectioners' sugar

¾ cup grated dark chocolate

Combine milk chocolate and coffee in the top of a double boiler over simmering water; stir until chocolate is melted. Transfer to a large bowl.

Beat butter into chocolate mixture; add egg yolks, one at a time, incorporating well.

Whisk in Chambord; set aside.

With a hand mixer, whip cream with 2 tablespoons of the confectioners' sugar in a large bowl until stiff peaks form; set aside. Clean beaters well.

In another large bowl, with the hand mixer, beat egg whites to soft peaks. Continue beating, adding remaining 2 tablespoons sugar, 1 tablespoon at a time, until stiff peaks form.

Fold chocolate mixture into egg whites; when almost incorporated, fold in whipped cream.

Fold in dark chocolate.

Pipe mousse into crystal champagne glasses or cocktail glasses, cover, and refrigerate until set, about 2 hours.

Makes 4 servings

Kitchen Notes

- Use a high-quality chocolate like Valrhona or Callebaut. It's worth the extra expense.

- A Microplane grater is great for grating chocolate as it keeps the chocolate from melting due to the heat created by the friction and ensures perfectly grated pieces.

- In order to more quickly and gently whip the cream, place the mixing bowl in the freezer for 30 minutes before whipping.

- Be sure to make the chocolate mousse in advance so it will have time to set before serving.

- Piping the mousse into the glasses rather than spooning it in gives it an especially pretty look and you don't need any special equipment. Cut off one corner of a large zip-top plastic bag. Place the mousse in the bag and pipe into the glasses.

Thyme-Baked Brie

"Let's face it, the French are far more sophisticated than we are when it comes to food. A typical dinner includes a cheese course at the end of the meal, and invariably you are faced with a tray of really interesting and delicious cheeses. Bess has never been a cheese fan, and I wondered how she would face the cheese platter every night of our 2-week trip. Surprisingly, not only was she immediately seduced by some of the subtler cheeses, she also fell in love with Epoisse, one of the more odorous ones. This Brie is a good cheese wrap-up to a meal when a selection of more artisanal cheeses is otherwise unavailable."

—John Currence

1 (16-ounce) package frozen puff pastry

Small (1-pound) wheel Brie (or other soft cheese)

2 teaspoons cracked black pepper

Leaves from 4 sprigs fresh thyme

1 large egg, lightly beaten

12 (¼-inch-thick) slices French bread, toasted lightly and buttered

1 small jar Major Grey's chutney

Let 1 sheet of puff pastry come to room temperature (typically there are two sheets in a package).

Preheat the oven to 425°F. Line a baking sheet with parchment paper or waxed paper.

Cut Brie into 4 pieces and refrigerate. Cut pastry into 4 squares large enough to wrap Brie quarters (about 4 by 4 inches). Sprinkle pastry with a little flour and roll out slightly (this will keep the dish from seeming like it has too much pastry).

Place a piece of Brie small enough to be totally wrapped in the pastry in the center of each pastry square. Sprinkle Brie with pepper and thyme. Turn Brie over and sprinkle again with pepper and thyme. Brush edges of pastry with beaten egg. Wrap pastry over the top of the Brie and seal well.

Place Brie (sealed side down, smooth side up) on prepared baking sheet. (If you like, decorate the top of the puff pastry with scrap pastry cut into a shape of your choice. Use egg as glue to attach shapes to pastry.)

Brush top of pastry with egg. Bake for 15 to 17 minutes, or until pastry is golden brown.

Serve with toasted French bread and chutney.

Makes 2 servings (with leftovers)

Kitchen Note

- This recipe is exceptional with Epoisse (a Burgundian soft cheese with an incredible nose), but Brie is perfectly acceptable.

Café Mocha for Two

The perfect ending to a delicious meal for two is to sip on a rich coffee drink flavored with a liqueur—in this case, crème de cacao. Relax and enjoy the warmth.

2 cups brewed Guatemalan coffee

2 teaspoons chocolate syrup

2 tablespoons crème de cacao

Homemade Whipped Cream (see recipe, below)

Shaved chocolate (see Kitchen Notes)

Pour brewed coffee into 2 coffee cups.

For each serving, add 1 teaspoon chocolate syrup and 1 tablespoon crème de cacao. Stir well.

Top each serving with Homemade Whipped Cream and shaved chocolate.

Homemade Whipped Cream

1 cup heavy cream, chilled

1 to 2 tablespoons confectioner's sugar

½ teaspoon vanilla

Chill a stainless steel bowl and beaters of a hand mixer in the freezer.

Pour cream into the chilled bowl. Beat with mixer on high speed until cream starts to thicken. Add confectioner's sugar and vanilla and beat until stiff peaks form.

Serve whipped cream as soon as possible. If it is made too far ahead, it will separate a bit.

Makes 2 cups

Kitchen Notes

- To shave chocolate into small curls, run a vegetable peeler down the side of a block of chilled chocolate.

- To grate chocolate, use a handheld Microplane grater. The fine side of a box grater is also good. It's best to grate chocolate just before using, as the fine pieces can easily lose their shape.

Variation

Grand Marnier Whipped Cream: You can add a bit of Grand Marnier to the whipped cream instead of the vanilla. This is good over fresh berries.

CHAPTER 15

Game Night Potluck

for 8 guests

Game night suppers should be hearty, healthy, and able to be served with ease to accommodate varying numbers at the table and ever-changing schedules. I was raised in a home with four brothers and a sister, all of whom were—and are—avid sports fans. Each of us was nurtured on sporting events starting in the crib, where the sounds of a Saturday baseball game on a transistor radio would lull us to sleep. Our father attended just about every major sporting event in the world from the World Series to the Olympics and has had at least one of us in tow at most of them. My brothers played sports, so pregame suppers were a part of everyday life. My mom knew just how to feed a group before a game with meals that were efficient and nutritious and that would stay with you whether you were a player or a spectator.

My son, Martin, plays trumpet in the school band, so game night suppers have become a new and pleasurable gathering at our house as well. As a "band mom," I was charged with the task of organizing home meals before football games. Martin told the entire band that his mom was cooking and it was going to be great. The pressure was on, and I knew just where to turn for advice: my younger brother, John. John and his talented wife, Susie, preside over a house full of four lively boys who play every imaginable sport 12 months a year. John is an active father who delights in participating in all his children's activities, as baseball commissioner, coach, or referee, and he's happiest with a carload of kids heading to some kind of game. He's always feeding a motley collection of kids and parents before a game, and his solution is to make it a potluck meal. John makes lasagna or a spaghetti pie and garlic bread and asks other parents to bring a dip, salad, and dessert. To speed things up, Susie suggests using large paper plates and napkins and serving cookies for dessert. She sets a festive table, coordinating paper products with the occasion or the season.

This menu is perfect for before-game suppers or evenings when friends gather for televised games. Roasted Red Pepper Spread is a colorful and delicious way to start any gathering. And it's quick and easy to make ahead because the peppers can be roasted in advance. It will keep for a week in the refrigerator—I like to use leftovers as a sandwich spread. The black bean salsa is guaranteed to please all ages and is best if it sits in the refrigerator overnight. The salsa travels well and is excellent for tailgating. White Chocolate Chunk Cookies are a favorite of John's four boys, and Susie makes them in bulk to take to out-of-town baseball tournaments and football games. The scrumptious caramel brownies are from my nephew's wife, Amanda Puckett, who has her own house full of boys. A hand-me-down recipe from her mother, the brownies are a winner with all ages and are requested at every family gathering.

Helping Hands

Help from the Seasoned Cook

Roasting red peppers is a job for an experienced cook.

Help from the Kids

Unwrapping the caramels for the brownies is a great job for kids, and they can assist with making the brownies and cookies as well. Kids can also take part in buttering the sliced French bread for the garlic bread.

Roasted Red Pepper Spread

2 large red bell peppers, roasted

4 ounces sun-dried tomatoes in oil (8 tomatoes), drained and diced

8 ounces cream cheese, at room temperature

1 bunch green onions, white parts coarsely chopped + 1 tablespoon green part, sliced on bias, for garnish

½ cup mayonnaise

½ cup sour cream

1 teaspoon Tabasco sauce

1½ teaspoons kosher salt

¾ teaspoon black pepper

Pita, toasted and cut into wedges, for dipping

Pulse peppers, tomatoes, cream cheese, chopped green onions, mayonnaise, sour cream, Tabasco, salt, and pepper in a food processor to a chunky consistency. Transfer to a serving bowl.

Garnish with sliced green onion and serve at room temperature with pita toasts fanned around the serving platter.

Makes 8 to 10 servings

Kitchen Note

- There are two common methods for roasting bell peppers: over the flame on a gas stove or under the broiler:

  Gas stove: Arrange the peppers on a wire rack or grid over a medium flame. Turn the peppers frequently until blackened evenly on all sides.

  Broiler: Broil peppers on the rack of a broiler pan 4 to 6 inches from the heat. Keep the oven door ajar. Turn to blacken evenly on all sides.

  Once blackened, rinse the peppers under cold water to help remove the charred skins.

Black Bean and Feta Salsa

¼ cup olive oil

¼ cup red wine vinegar

½ to 1 teaspoon cayenne pepper

2 (15-ounce) cans black beans, drained and rinsed

1¼ cups fresh or frozen corn kernels

1 bunch green onions, chopped

1 green bell pepper, seeded and finely chopped

1 red bell pepper, seeded and finely chopped

1 tomato, chopped

Garlic salt

8 ounces feta cheese, crumbled

Tortilla chips for serving

Whisk together olive oil, vinegar, and cayenne in a bowl.

Combine black beans, corn, green onions, bell peppers, and tomato in a large bowl and mix well.

Add vinegar mixture and mix well. Stir in garlic salt to taste. Sprinkle with crumbled feta.

Serve with tortilla chips.

Makes 8 to 10 servings

Kitchen Note

● This salsa is also delicious served as a side salad with poultry, fish, or meat dishes.

● Make the salsa the night before you plan to serve it, so the flavors will be more robust.

Good Luck Pizza Dip

This is a favorite of all pizza lovers. It is the most requested dip for pregame band dinners and football dinners at St. Andrew's Episcopal School in Ridgeland, Mississippi.

1 onion, chopped

½ medium green bell pepper, seeded and diced

1 tablespoon olive oil

8 ounces cream cheese, softened

1 (14-ounce) jar pizza sauce

¼ pound pepperoni slices, cut in half

1 (6-ounce) can black olives, drained and sliced

2 cups shredded mozzarella cheese

  Corn chips for dipping

Preheat the oven to 400°F. Coat a 9-inch glass baking dish with cooking spray.

Sauté onion and pepper in olive oil in a medium skillet over medium heat until softened; remove from the heat.

Spread cream cheese on the bottom of the prepared baking dish and top evenly with onion mixture.

Pour pizza sauce over onion mixture and spread to an even layer.

Top with pepperoni and olives. Sprinkle with mozzarella cheese.

Bake, uncovered, for 20 minutes, or until heated through. Serve with corn chips.

Makes 8 servings

Old-Fashioned Lasagna

Meat Sauce

- 1 pound sweet or hot Italian sausages (about 5 links), casings removed and meat crumbled
- ½ pound ground beef
- ½ cup finely chopped onion
- 2 cloves garlic, minced
- 2 tablespoons sugar
- 1½ teaspoons dried basil
- ½ teaspoon ground fennel seed
- 1½ teaspoons salt
- ½ teaspoon black pepper
- 4 cups canned tomatoes, with juices
- 1 (6-ounce) can tomato paste
- 2 tablespoons finely chopped fresh parsley

Ricotta Mixture

- 1 (15-ounce) container ricotta cheese, drained
- 1 large egg
- 2 tablespoons finely chopped fresh parsley
- ½ teaspoon salt

Lasagna

- 12 lasagna noodles
- ¾ pound mozzarella cheese, thinly sliced
- ¾ cup freshly grated Parmesan cheese

To make meat sauce: In a large saucepan over medium heat, cook sausage and beef until browned. Drain fat and return meat to the pan.

Add onion and cook until softened, 4 to 5 minutes. Add garlic and cook, stirring frequently, for 30 seconds to 1 minute longer, or until garlic is just softened but not browned.

Add sugar, basil, fennel seed, salt, and pepper and mix well.

Add tomatoes and their juices, tomato paste, and ½ cup water, mashing tomatoes with back of a wooden spoon.

Bring to a boil and reduce heat. Cover and simmer, stirring occasionally, until thickened, 10 to 15 minutes. Stir in parsley and remove from the heat.

To make ricotta mixture: In a medium bowl, combine ricotta, egg, parsley, and salt; mix well.

To assemble lasagna: Preheat the oven to 375°F.

In an 8-quart pot, bring 6 quarts of lightly salted water to a boil. Add noodles, 2 or 3 at a time. Return to a boil. Cook, uncovered, stirring occasionally, for 10 minutes, or until noodles are just tender. Drain noodles in a colander and rinse under cold water. Dry on paper towels.

Spoon 1½ cups of meat sauce into the bottom of a 9- by 13-inch baking dish.

Top with 4 of the noodles, placing lengthwise and overlapping, to cover. Spread with half of the ricotta mixture; top with one-third of the mozzarella. Spoon another 1½ cups of meat sauce over cheese and sprinkle with ¼ cup of Parmesan.

Repeat layering.

Spread remaining sauce on top; sprinkle with remaining mozzarella and Parmesan.

Cover with foil and bake for 35 minutes. Remove foil and bake for 15 minutes longer, or until bubbly and golden brown.

Cool for 15 minutes in the pan before serving.

Cut into squares with a sharp knife. Use a wide spatula to serve.

Makes 8 to 10 servings

Kitchen Notes

- The noodles should be cooked until just tender, not soft. They will cook more in the oven.
- If the baking dish is very full, place a baking sheet underneath when baking to catch drips.

Spaghetti Pie

Filling

1 pound ground beef

½ cup chopped onion

1 (15-ounce) can tomato sauce

1 (6-ounce) can tomato paste

¼ cup white wine

1 teaspoon sugar

1½ teaspoons dried basil

1 teaspoon dried oregano

Salt and black pepper

Spaghetti Mixture

6 ounces thin spaghetti, cooked according to package directions until al dente, then drained

1 tablespoon fresh basil or 1 teaspoon dried basil

½ cup grated Parmesan cheese

4 tablespoons unsalted butter, softened

1 large egg, beaten

½ medium clove garlic, minced

1 cup ricotta cheese

1 cup shredded mozzarella cheese

1 teaspoon minced flat-leaf parsley for garnish (optional)

To make filling: Cook ground beef and onion in large skillet over medium heat until beef is browned. Drain off fat and return beef and onion to the pan.

Stir in tomato sauce, tomato paste, wine, sugar, basil, oregano, salt, and pepper. Heat thoroughly, then remove from the heat.

To make spaghetti mixture: In a large bowl, toss spaghetti with basil, mixing well. Stir in Parmesan, butter, egg, and garlic.

With two sharp knives, chop mixture into 1-inch pieces.

To assemble pie: Preheat the oven to 350°F. Grease a 10-inch pie plate.

Spread ¼ inch of the filling onto the bottom of the pie plate. Press spaghetti mixture into plate to make a "crust." Spread ricotta cheese on crust and top with remaining filling.

Bake for 20 minutes. Sprinkle with mozzarella cheese and bake for 10 minutes longer, or until the mozzarella melts.

Cool in pan for 10 to 15 minutes.

Garnish with minced parsley, if using, and serve.

Makes 8 servings

Kitchen Note

- We like to make individual spaghetti pies and freeze them. If you plan do so, make the pies in little individual throwaway potpie tins and don't bake them; instead wrap tightly and label with the date before freezing. To serve, defrost the pies to room temperature, then bake in a preheated 350°F oven for 20 minutes, or until heated through.

Mixed Greens with Toasted Walnuts and Honey Mustard Vinaigrette

Honey Mustard Vinaigrette

¼ cup honey mustard

1 tablespoon honey

1 tablespoon balsamic vinegar

1 teaspoon sugar

1 teaspoon kosher salt

½ teaspoon black pepper

½ cup extra-virgin olive oil

Salad

2 (10-ounce) bag mixed greens

1 cup crumbled feta cheese

1 cup golden raisins

½ cup toasted walnuts or pine nuts

To make vinaigrette: In a medium bowl, whisk honey mustard, honey, vinegar, sugar, salt, and pepper until combined.

Slowly drizzle in olive oil, whisking constantly, until emulsified.

To make salad: In a serving bowl, combine greens, feta, raisins, and walnuts.

Pour enough vinaigrette over salad to just coat greens and toss.

Makes 8 servings

Kitchen Note

● **To toast walnuts or pine nuts:** In a small bowl, toss the nuts with a little bit of oil and salt, and then place them in a single layer on a baking sheet. Toast in 300°F oven for 15 to 20 minutes, or until lightly browned.

Garlic Bread

1 loaf French bread

½ cup unsalted butter

2 or 3 cloves garlic, crushed or minced

3 to 4 teaspoons chopped fresh parsley

Preheat the oven to 350°F.

Cut bread lengthwise into halves.

Melt butter in a small skillet and add garlic. Stir well and remove from the heat.

Brush butter mixture over the cut sides of the bread halves and sprinkle with parsley.

Place the two halves on a baking sheet and bake for 10 minutes, or until crisp.

Slice as desired and serve.

Makes 8 to 10 servings

Kitchen Note

- To make the garlic bread ahead, slice and butter it and wrap it in foil until ready to bake.

Warm Vegetable Garlic Bread

½ cup unsalted butter

3 tablespoons olive oil

1 cup shredded carrots

1 cup shredded zucchini

5 to 6 garlic cloves, minced

1 loaf Italian bread or French bread

¾ cup freshly grated Parmesan cheese

Preheat the oven to 350°F.

In a small skillet, heat butter and oil over medium heat. Add carrots, zucchini, and garlic and cook, stirring occasionally, until tender, 5 to 7 minutes.

Meanwhile, slice bread in half lengthwise.

Spread hot vegetable mixture on each half and sprinkle with Parmesan cheese.

Put halves back together and wrap in foil. Bake for 20 to 25 minutes, or until heated through.

Makes 8 to 10 servings.

White Chocolate Chunk Cookies

1 cup vegetable shortening

¾ cup firmly packed brown sugar

¾ cup granulated sugar

3 large eggs

1 teaspoon vanilla extract

1½ cups all-purpose flour

1 teaspoon baking powder

1 teaspoon baking soda

½ teaspoon salt

2 (6-ounce) white chocolate baking bars, cut into ¼-inch chunks

1 cup sweetened flaked coconut

½ cup old-fashioned rolled oats

½ cup coarsely chopped walnuts

Preheat the oven to 325°F.

In a large bowl, cream shortening, brown sugar, and granulated sugar until light and fluffy.

Add eggs, one at a time, beating well after each addition. Add vanilla and blend well.

In another large bowl, stir together flour, baking powder, baking soda, and salt. Add to sugar mixture, mixing well.

Stir in white chocolate, coconut, oats, and walnuts.

Drop by rounded tablespoons, 2 inches apart, onto ungreased baking sheets.

Bake for 8 to 10 minutes, or until light golden brown.

Let cool on the baking sheets, then transfer to racks to cool completely.

Makes 4 dozen cookies

Kitchen Note

- One 10-ounce package of white chocolate baking pieces or a 12-ounce package of vanilla milk chocolate chips can be substituted for the baking bars. Do not substitute almond bark or vanilla-flavored candy coating.

Amanda's Caramel Brownies

"This recipe has been handed down from my mom, Karen Bush. They are always a hit and are requested at every party, girls' get-together, holiday, and family gathering and enjoyed by all ages—the young and the young-at-heart."

—Amanda Puckett

1 (14-ounce) bag caramels, unwrapped

⅔ cup evaporated milk

1 (18.25-ounce) box German chocolate cake mix

¾ cup unsalted butter, melted

1 (6-ounce) package semisweet chocolate chips

Preheat the oven to 350°F. Grease a 9- by 13-inch baking pan.

In the top of a double boiler over simmering water, melt caramels in ⅓ cup of the evaporated milk. Mix well and set aside.

In a large bowl, combine cake mix, butter, and remaining ⅓ cup evaporated milk. Mix well.

Press half of the cake mixture into the prepared baking pan.

Bake for 6 minutes.

Remove the pan from the oven and layer chocolate chips, then caramel mixture, then remaining cake mixture on top.

Return to the oven and bake for 15 to 18 minutes longer, or until firm.

Cool in the pan, then refrigerate for at least 2 hours before cutting.

Makes 2 dozen brownies

CHAPTER 16

Tree-Trimming Party

for 8 guests

Gathering friends and family for a tree-trimming party sets a festive mood for the holiday season. This party tradition began when I lived in Southern California, far from my Deep South roots and homesick for family. Never one to accept the idea of being a long-distance grandparent, my father would fly out to California on the first Tuesday of December for the sole purpose of taking my young son, Martin, and me to get our Christmas tree. He would wait patiently while we found the perfect tree, then help us string the lights and decorate. Parents and kids at Martin's school clamored to meet the mysterious granddaddy who flew from Mississippi to get a Christmas tree. It seemed the perfect excuse for a party, so I invited parents and kids to meet my dad and join in the merriment as we decorated our tree.

When we moved home to Mississippi several years later, Martin asked if granddaddy was still going to take us to get our Christmas tree and if there were tree-trimming parties in Mississippi. Yes, to both. Now it's a 15-year tradition for grandfather and grandson, and they always bring home the "perfect" tree. As technology has changed, so has my tree-trimming party. I still plan the food and festivities, but now I e-mail both menu and recipes to my friends so they can choose what they want to cook. This chapter tells you how to create a magical holiday party with a little advance planning and by doing what I do best—keeping it simple.

I enjoy involving revelers of every age in the party preparation and this menu allows you to include even the youngest ones, who can begin preparing for the party weeks ahead by stringing cranberries and popcorn to trim the tree.

When friends ask, "What can I bring?" I've learned over the years to graciously accept all offers. The party is more fun and the holiday spirit is always enhanced when we take the time to involve others.

Partygoers of all ages will enjoy these recipes, which have been graciously shared by friends and family who have participated in my parties over the years.

Betty Allin's Confetti Crab Dip is colorful, delicious, and good for a crowd any time of year. For a variation, I sometimes roast the peppers, which adds a deep, smoky flavor. Chopping everything the day before makes it a breeze to assemble this tasty dip.

Holiday Holly doubles as a delicious sweet treat and a colorful garnish. A favorite in my cooking classes, it was passed along to me by Jane Brock, a legendary cook and entertainer in my hometown with a flair for creating whimsical recipes like this one.

Making Ooey-Gooey Fudge is an annual ritual for Martin and me. A plate of this delicious fudge is a popular gift for friends, neighbors, and teachers. Another favorite gift from our kitchen is the sugar cookie dough, wrapped in red or green cellophane and tied with holiday ribbon. Present it along with the icing recipe and a cookie cutter. I get a jump on the busy holiday season by starting to make my Christmas cookie dough right after Thanksgiving, as it freezes beautifully.

When my family gathers for our holiday celebration there are more than 30 of us to feed. With an age range from 7 months to 70 years, the main course has to be easy to prepare, easy to serve, and something that all ages will enjoy. Enchiladas fit the bill on all accounts and have become a mainstay of our annual family celebration and my tree-trimming parties. I make both kinds a day ahead in multiple 9- by 13-inch dishes so they'll be easy to refrigerate, then whisk into the oven.

Helping Hands

Help from the Seasoned Cook

Have a seasoned cook help you with the sauces and prepping for the enchiladas. The sauces and other enchilada ingredients can be prepped the day before, leaving only the assembly to be done on the day of your gathering. Keep in mind that the shrimp needs to marinate for 1 to 2 hours before grilling and the fudge sets for an hour.

Help from the Kids

After making and rolling out the dough, leave the cutting of the Very Merry Sugar Cookies to the kids and you will be amazed at their creations. While the kids have the cookie cutters out, let them make Ho Ho Sandwiches: Have them cut out shapes from sandwich bread of your choice with the holiday cookie cutters. Fill with fillings the kids and adults like and place the sandwiches on a platter for everyone to enjoy. They can save the crusts from the bread to feed the birds.

Confetti Crab Dip

This dip makes a beautiful presentation on a festive platter and will likely serve more than 8 guests. Leftovers will keep for a day in the refrigerator.

2 8-ounce packages cream cheese, softened

2 tablespoons Worcestershire sauce

4 teaspoons Tabasco sauce

3 to 4 cloves garlic, crushed

1 (12-ounce) bottle Heinz cocktail sauce

1 pound lump crabmeat, picked through to remove any pieces of shell

8 ounces mozzarella cheese, shredded

2 tomatoes, chopped

½ cup chopped green onions

2 small bell peppers (red, green, yellow, or a combination), seeded and chopped

Unsalted wafers or crackers, for serving

Combine cream cheese, Worcestershire, Tabasco, and garlic in a medium bowl. Spread out on a large serving dish into a 12- to 16-inch circle.

Pour cocktail sauce over cream cheese mixture. Top with crabmeat. Sprinkle mozzarella over crabmeat.

Combine tomatoes, green onions, and peppers in a small bowl. Sprinkle over mozzarella.

Serve with wafers.

Makes 12 to 16 servings

Kitchen Notes

- If you like, make the dip early in the day and cover and refrigerate. It will ooze around the edges; wipe this up with paper towels.
- If you feel like roasting some bell peppers (see Kitchen Note on page 163), they add a nice smokiness to the dip.
- This dip is great at any time of year.

Sweet and Sour Meatballs

1 pound ground beef

1 (2-ounce) envelope Lipton onion soup mix

1 large egg

¼ cup seasoned Italian breadcrumbs

1 (14-ounce) bottle Heinz hot ketchup

1 (14-ounce) bottle regular ketchup

1 (10-ounce) jar currant jelly

Preheat the oven to 350°F.

Combine beef, soup mix, egg, and bread crumbs in a large bowl. Shape into 24 small meatballs.

Place meatballs on a wire rack set on a baking sheet. Bake for 20 to 25 minutes, or until cooked through.

Combine hot ketchup, regular ketchup, and jelly in a saucepan over medium heat. Cook, stirring, until jelly is melted.

Transfer meatballs and sauce to a chafing dish and serve immediately.

Makes 24 meatballs

Grilled Shrimp Enchiladas with Cranberry Orange Sauce

Shrimp and Marinade

½ cup olive oil

Juice of 1 lemon

Juice of 1 lime

Juice of 1 tangerine or orange

¼ bunch cilantro, chopped

1½ pounds large shrimp, peeled and deveined

Cranberry Orange Sauce

3 oranges, peeled, sectioned, and seeded

2 cups cranberries, washed

½ bunch cilantro

¼ cup sugar

Juice of 1 lime

1 tablespoon chili paste

Enchiladas

2 tablespoons chili paste, approximately

1 medium onion, chopped

1 tablespoon unsalted butter

3 cloves garlic, minced

2 cups shredded pepper Jack cheese

2 roasted red bell peppers, cut into thin strips

¼ cup packed cilantro leaves, chopped

10 (8-inch) corn tortillas

To marinate and grill shrimp: In a large bowl, whisk together olive oil, lemon juice, lime juice, tangerine juice, and cilantro. Add shrimp and toss to coat. Cover and marinate in the refrigerator for 1 to 2 hours.

Heat a barbecue grill to hot or preheat the broiler.

Remove shrimp from marinade and discard marinade. Grill shrimp for 3 minutes per side, or broil for 3 to 5 minutes per side, or until cooked through. Let shrimp cool, then cut in half.

To make cranberry orange sauce: Pulse all sauce ingredients in a food processor until finely chopped. Transfer to a bowl.

To make enchiladas: Preheat the oven to 350°F. Cover the bottom of a 9- by 13-inch baking pan with 1 tablespoon of the chili paste.

In a medium nonstick skillet, sauté onion in butter over medium heat until softened, about 5 minutes. Add garlic and cook for 2 minutes longer. Remove the pan from the heat.

In a large bowl, combine grilled shrimp, onion, garlic, 1¼ cups of the cheese, the peppers, and cilantro and mix thoroughly.

Brush one side of a tortilla lightly with chili paste. Place ¼ cup loosely packed shrimp mixture in the center of the tortilla and roll tightly. Place seam side down in the prepared pan. Repeat to make remaining enchiladas.

Top enchiladas with cranberry orange sauce. Bake for 20 minutes, or until heated through. Scatter remaining ¾ cup cheese over all. Return to oven and bake for 5 to 7 minutes, or until cheese is melted.

Makes 10 enchiladas

Chicken Enchiladas with Caramelized Onion and Green Chile Sauce

Chicken Filling

2 tablespoons unsalted butter

2 large onions, thinly sliced

3 to 4 cups chopped cooked chicken breast

8 ounces cream cheese

Salt and black pepper

Green Chile Sauce

2 cups canned diced green chiles, drained

½ cup chopped onion

2 garlic cloves, minced

1 tablespoon dried cumin

1 tablespoon dried oregano

½ teaspoon sugar

1 (14-ounce) can chicken broth

½ cup tomatillo salsa

Enchiladas

10 (8-inch) flour tortillas

2 cups shredded pepper Jack cheese

To make filling: Melt butter in a large skillet over medium-low heat. Add onions and sauté until lightly browned and caramelized, about 20 minutes.

Reduce heat to low; add chicken and cream cheese, stirring until blended. Season with salt and pepper and remove from the heat.

To make chile sauce: Pulse chiles, onion, garlic, cumin, oregano, and sugar in a food processor several times just to blend.

Combine green chile mixture and chicken broth in a medium saucepan and bring to a boil. Boil until slightly reduced to the consistency of a thin gravy, about 5 minutes. Season with salt, if desired. Stir salsa into green chile mixture and remove from the heat.

To make enchiladas: Preheat the oven to 350°F. Pour enough chile sauce into a 9- by 13-inch baking dish to cover the bottom.

Spoon ⅓ cup chicken filling down the center of a tortilla and roll up. Place seam side down in the baking dish. Repeat with remaining filling and tortillas to make enchiladas.

Pour remaining chile sauce over the top and sprinkle with cheese.

Bake for 20 minutes, or until cheese melts and enchiladas are heated through.

Makes 10 enchiladas

Grilled Shrimp Enchiladas with Cranberry Orange Sauce
(page 178) and Chicken Enchiladas with Caramelized Onion
and Green Chile Sauce (opposite)

Reindeer Rice

½ cup unsalted butter

3 carrots, finely diced

1 small onion, finely chopped

2 stalks celery, finely diced

1½ cups white rice

2 (10¾-ounce) cans beef consommé or broth

Preheat the oven to 350°F.

In a medium saucepan, melt butter over medium heat. Add carrots, onion, and celery and sauté until softened, about 7 minutes.

Add rice and continue to cook for 2 to 3 minutes longer.

Combine consommé and enough water in a large measuring cup to make enough liquid for cooking rice per package instructions (you'll need about 3 cups). Stir into vegetables and rice.

Pour rice mixture into a 2-quart baking dish. Cover and bake for 1 hour, or until rice is tender and all liquid is absorbed.

Makes 8 servings

Lemon Herb Rice

● Substitute 2½ cups of chicken stock for the beef consommé. Omit the carrots and add 1 minced clove of garlic, 1½ tablespoons of grated lemon zest, and 2 tablespoons of chopped fresh dill.

● My friend Gayden Metcalfe, author of *Being Dead Is No Excuse*, says "If you have your own chicken stock, made from scratch, you will be assured of an especially delicious dish. Canned chicken stock is OK, but your final product is just not as rich and flavorsome."

Feliz Navidad Salad

Dressing

1 teaspoon grated lemon zest

1 teaspoon grated orange zest

2 tablespoons lemon juice

2 tablespoons orange juice

1 tablespoon sherry vinegar

1 clove garlic, finely chopped

1 teaspoon ground cumin, or more to taste

½ teaspoon paprika

½ teaspoon salt

½ cup vegetable oil

2 tablespoons chopped cilantro

1 jalapeño chile pepper, seeded and finely chopped (optional)

Salad

6 cups fresh field greens

1 jicama, peeled, sliced, and julienned

1 large red bell pepper, seeded and diced

1 large yellow bell pepper, seeded and diced

1 red onion, diced

1 (14-ounce) can hearts of palm, sliced

4 oranges, peeled and sectioned, or 1 (14-ounce) can mandarin oranges, drained

To make dressing: Combine zests, juices, vinegar, garlic, cumin, paprika, and salt in a small bowl.

Slowly whisk in oil.

Taste and add more juice or oil to balance dressing. Stir in cilantro and jalapeño.

Blend and adjusting seasonings.

To make salad: In a large serving bowl, combine greens, jicama, peppers, onion, and hearts of palm.

Pour enough dressing over salad to coat greens and toss well.

Top with orange sections, toss gently, and serve.

Makes 8 servings

Ooey-Gooey Fudge

My mother was known to bribe her own tribe of children and their houseful of friends with the promise of Ooey-Gooey Fudge. This recipe is simple to prepare and a fun way to involve young cooks.

4½ cups sugar

1 (13-ounce) can evaporated milk

1 cup unsalted butter

¾ teaspoon salt

3 (12-ounce) packages semisweet chocolate chips

1 (7-ounce) jar marshmallow creme

4 cups chopped pecans

Grease 9- by 13-inch glass baking dish.

In a large saucepan, combine sugar, evaporated milk, butter, and salt. Mix well.

Bring to a boil and reduce the heat to medium. Continue to cook at a low boil for 9 minutes, stirring constantly. Remove the pan from the heat.

Immediately add chocolate chips and stir until melted. Add marshmallow creme and pecans. Mix well.

Pour mixture into the prepared baking dish. Let stand until fudge is set, at least 1 hour.

Makes 4 dozen small pieces

Kitchen Note

● People think fudge is difficult to make, but this version is easy. Use some for your gathering and give some as gifts to neighbors and teachers. It will keep for up to a week in the refrigerator, but it becomes harder to cut.

Holiday Holly

30 large marshmallows

½ cup unsalted butter

1½ teaspoons green food coloring

3 cups cornflakes

Red Hots candies

Melt marshmallows and butter in the top of a double boiler over simmering water. Stir in food coloring. Remove from the heat.

Add cornflakes and stir just to cover the cornflakes. Be careful not to crush flakes.

Drop by teaspoons and tablespoons (to vary sizes) onto wax paper. Decorate with candies before the holly sets.

Makes 2 dozen treats

Kitchen Notes

- These bright green treats are a favorite with little ones. The oohs and ahhs you get as the cornflakes turn green will delight young and old.

- Do not do this on a rainy day or the holly will become sticky.

- Do not put them in a tin box or in any closed container or they will become gummy; they need to "breathe."

Peppermint Hot Chocolate

This recipe is for one mug of hot chocolate. To make more, simply heat more milk, then put the same amount of sugar, cocoa powder, and vanilla in each mug, as indicated below.

1⅓ cups milk

2 tablespoons sugar

1 tablespoon unsweetened cocoa powder

⅛ teaspoon vanilla extract

Whipped cream

Peppermint candy canes

In a saucepan over low heat, warm milk until tiny bubbles appear around the edges of the pan. Remove the pan from the heat.

Place the sugar, cocoa powder, and vanilla in a mug and stir to combine. Add 1 tablespoon hot milk to the cocoa mixture and stir until it is smooth with no visible lumps.

Pour the remaining hot milk into the mug. Stir well, top with whipped cream, and add a peppermint candy cane to use as a stirrer. Serve immediately.

Makes 1 serving

Very Merry Sugar Cookies
with Our Favorite Buttercream Frosting

Cookies

1 cup unsalted butter, softened

2 cups granulated sugar

3 large eggs

2 teaspoons vanilla extract

4 cups sifted all-purpose flour

2 teaspoons baking powder

Colored or white sugar for sprinkling, optional

Frosting

1 (16-ounce) box confectioners' sugar

½ cup unsalted butter, softened

2 tablespoons milk

2 teaspoons vanilla extract

Food coloring of your choice, optional

For the cookies: Preheat the oven to 350°F. Line 2 baking sheets with parchment paper.

Cream butter and sugar together in a large bowl.

Stir in eggs and vanilla and beat until fluffy.

Stir in flour and baking powder until well combined.

Place dough on a large piece of floured parchment paper and coat with flour. Enclose dough tightly in parchment and refrigerate until dough is quite firm, about 1 hour.

Roll out about one-fourth of dough at a time on a lightly floured board to about ⅛ inch thick. Do not overwork dough or it will stick to the board.

Cut out cookies with holiday cookie cutters. Transfer shapes to prepared baking sheets.

Sprinkle with colored or white sugar, if you like.

Bake for about 10 minutes, or until cookies are lightly browned.

Let cool slightly on the baking sheets, then transfer to wire racks to cool completely.

Repeat with remaining dough.

For the frosting: In a large bowl, beat together sugar, butter, milk, and vanilla until smooth. If necessary, add more milk until frosting is spreading consistency.

If desired, add a few drops of food coloring and stir to blend. Use to frost cookies.

Makes about 6½ dozen cookies and 2 cups frosting

Holiday Holly (page 185), Very Merry Sugar Cookies with Our Favorite Buttercream Frosting (opposite), and Peppermint Hot Chocolate (page 185)

Made from Scratch

I inherited both my grandmother Helen's name and her love of baking. And anyone who knows me well knows about my grandmother's pound cake. I've carried many a cake across the country and even sealed a book deal with one.

Often when I would visit, the dough for Grandmother's rolls would be rising in the refrigerator; there would be a pound cake in the oven and her Sunbeam mixer going full speed. She laughed when I asked her why her mixer was still running when the cake was already in the oven. The fact is, she was never content to be a one-cake cook and the second cake (an angel food cake) took patience to make. When we sat down together to have some, it was fluffy, delicious, and so light that it almost melted in my mouth. Granddaddy would put fresh peach slices, strawberries, or fresh blueberries on top. I had never made my grandmother's angel food cake until a recent Sunday morning. Her handwritten recipe was scribbled with funny little notes about cooling the cake over a Coke bottle and I learned firsthand why this is a cake that requires patience. My plan was to make the cake before church and let it cool for the recommended 2 hours—just in time for it to be a spectacular end to Sunday lunch. Well, I never made it to church because my mixer, like her old Sunbeam, had to work overtime beating the egg whites to form stiff peaks. Angel food cake, popularized in the 1800s before the advent of the electric mixer, does not contain a single bit of fat. Sugar is needed not only for taste but also to keep the egg whites lofty enough to hold the rest of the ingredients. Although my son and I agreed that the cake would fall out of the pan if we removed it from the oven and perched it upside down on a Coke bottle, we took my grandmother's advice. With no Coke bottle to be found, we used a wine bottle and waited for the cake to fall out . . . but it did not. We ended up with a beautiful angel food cake on our cake stand and a morning full of memories and laughter while making it.

I write my cookbooks in menu style and always have so many good dessert recipes that I can't fit them all in. That's my grandmother's spirit in me. For me, working with flour and rolling out dough is one of the most enjoyable things I do. I haven't found many life situations that can't be improved with a pound cake or a pie. This chapter is a tribute to my grandmother, who has inspired me and has taught me that baking is about love and, most importantly, patience. The lessons I have learned over the years while the mixer is running or the dough is rising are life lessons. The conversations that I've had with my son while he was helping me sift flour or crack eggs are ones that I treasure. In this chapter, you'll find not only wonderful recipes for cakes, cookies, and pies but also recipes for life. There is nothing more wonderful than a gift made from scratch.

Lemon Chiffon Pie
with Cornflake Crust

Cornflake Crust

4 cups cornflakes

4 tablespoons unsalted butter, melted

¼ cup sugar

½ teaspoon ground cinnamon

Filling

1 (¾-ounce) envelope unflavored gelatin

⅛ teaspoon salt

4 large eggs, separated (see Kitchen Note, below)

1 (6-ounce) can frozen lemonade concentrate, (not defrosted)

½ cup sugar

To make crust: Preheat the oven to 350°F.

Roll cornflakes in a plastic bag with a rolling pin to make 1 cup fine crumbs.

Combine cornflake crumbs with melted butter, sugar, and cinnamon.

Press firmly into an 8-inch pie plate. Bake for 8 to 10 minutes, or until lightly browned.

To make filling: Sprinkle gelatin over ½ cup cold water in a saucepan . Add salt and egg yolks and mix well.

Place over low heat and cook, stirring constantly, until mixture thickens slightly and gelatin dissolves, 3 to 4 minutes. Remove from heat.

Add lemonade concentrate and stir until melted.

In a very clean bowl, beat egg whites with an electric mixer on high speed until soft peaks form. Gradually add sugar, beating until stiff peaks form. Fold in gelatin mixture.

Scrape filling into pie shell. Cover and refrigerate for 3 hours before serving.

Makes 8 servings

Kitchen Note

- If you like, use egg white powder (dried egg whites) for the uncooked whites in this recipe. It can be reconstituted with water and the reconstituted powder whips up just like the whites themselves. And because the powder is pasteurized, it can be used safely without cooking it. For each egg white, you will need 2 level teaspoons of powdered egg white plus 2 tablespoons of water.

Clara Nestor's Perfect Pecan Pie

Mrs. Nestor, my friend Marsha's mother, makes this tasty pie for every occasion. It freezes beautifully, so she always keeps one on standby in the freezer. Living in a pecan-growing area, she gathers her pecans in the fall, then shells and freezes them so she'll always have some on hand.

1½ cups sugar

½ cup unsalted butter

½ cup light corn syrup

3 large eggs, lightly beaten

1½ cups pecans

1 teaspoon vanilla extract

½ recipe The Best Pie Crust (page 194)

Whipped cream for serving (optional)

Preheat the oven to 375°F.

In a saucepan, melt sugar, butter, and corn syrup over low heat. Do not boil. Remove from heat.

Stir in eggs until well mixed.

In food processor, chop pecans to desired consistency.

Fold pecans and vanilla into butter mixture.

Fit rolled-out dough into a 9-inch pie plate.

Pour mixture into pie shell.

Bake for 40 to 45 minutes, or until the center is firm when the pie is gently shaken. Serve with whipped cream if you like.

Makes 8 servings

Kitchen Note

- If you plan to freeze the pie, or an extra one, double wrap it in plastic wrap and freeze for up to a month.

The Best Pie Crust

This pie crust recipe is also from the kitchen of Clara Nestor.

2 cups + 2 tablespoons sifted all-purpose flour

¾ teaspoon salt

⅔ cups vegetable shortening (Crisco)

3 tablespoons ice water

Mix flour and salt together in a large bowl. Cut in shortening with a pastry blender.

Drizzle ice water into mixture a tablespoon at a time while pulling dough with a fork from edge of bowl to center, until mixture is equally moistened.

Divide the dough in half. With floured hands, form balls with dough.

Roll out on floured board to make 2 (9-inch) crusts.

Makes enough dough for 2 (9-inch) pie crusts

Kitchen Notes

- If you do not have a pastry blender, cut the flour into the shortening with two table knives.

- The dough should form a ball that is firm and not too wet.

- Always use ice water and the least amount of handling for a flakier crust.

- When rolling out, remember to press down on the dough with the rolling pin and start in the center of the ball, rolling out to the north, south, east, and west.

- Pies generally cook at a fairly high temperature and the edges of the crust can get brown before the pie is cooked in the center. Attaching 3-inch strips of aluminum foil together to form a collar and placing it around the edge of the crust when it is golden brown will prevent it from browning any further.

Pumpkin Chiffon Pie

This pie is a lighter version of a traditional pumpkin pie and is perfect after a heavy meal. It has been passed down through many generations in my family. My grandmother told me to always make two—one for my family and one to give to a friend or neighbor. I usually take one to my brother Richard at Thanksgiving, as this is his favorite.

½ recipe The Best Pie Crust (opposite)

1 (¾-ounce) envelope gelatin

3 large eggs, separated (see Kitchen Note, page 191)

1 cup sugar

1¼ cups pumpkin puree (not pumpkin pie filling)

½ cup milk

1 teaspoon ground cinnamon

1 teaspoon ground nutmeg

½ teaspoon ground ginger

½ teaspoon salt

Preheat the oven to 300°F.

Fit rolled-out dough into a 9-inch pie pan.

Bake for 10 to 12 minutes, or until lightly browned.

Dissolve gelatin in ¼ cup water; set aside.

Beat egg yolks in the top of a double boiler over simmering water.

Stir in ½ cup of the sugar, the pumpkin, and milk. Cook, stirring occasionally, until thickened, about 10 minutes.

Stir in gelatin mixture, cinnamon, nutmeg, ginger, and salt. Remove from the heat and let cool.

In a very clean bowl, beat egg whites with an electric mixer on high speed until soft peaks form. Gradually add remaining ½ cup sugar, beating until stiff peaks form.

Fold egg whites into pumpkin mixture. Scrape into pie shell.

Cover and refrigerate for 3 hours before serving.

Makes 8 servings

Kitchen Note

- To fold one mixture into another, use a whisk, a large spoon, or a rubber spatula and gently work the ingredients together in a figure-eight motion. Turn the bowl slowly, working quickly and stopping when no streaks remain. The idea is to release as few air bubbles as possible, creating a lighter result.

Mom's Banana Pudding

I found this recipe in my mom's own personal date book from 1954.

⅔ cup + ¼ cup sugar

5 tablespoons all-purpose flour

¼ teaspoon kosher salt

2 cups whole milk

2 large eggs, separated

1 teaspoon vanilla extract

5 medium-ripe bananas, cut into ¼-inch-thick slices

40 to 45 vanilla wafers

Preheat the oven to 350°F.

Combine ⅔ cup of the sugar with the flour and salt in the top of a double boiler over simmering water. Stir in milk gradually and cook, stirring until thick.

Blend in egg yolks and cook a minute longer. Cool and add vanilla.

Place a small amount of custard on the bottom of 1½-quart casserole dish. Cover with a layer of sliced bananas, and then a layer of vanilla wafers. Continue to make 3 layers, ending with custard.

In a very clean bowl, beat egg whites with an electric mixer on high speed until soft peaks form. Gradually add remaining ¼ cup sugar, beating until stiff peaks form.

Spoon egg white mixture over custard; spread evenly to cover entire surface of custard.

Bake for 15 minutes, or until lightly golden browned.

Makes 8 servings

Kitchen Notes

- Don't throw out those overripe bananas! They're perfect for using in bread recipes or for making a smoothie. Freeze them in sealable plastic freezer bags and thaw them slightly when ready to use.

- Always chill the bowl and beaters before beating egg whites or whipping cream.

Dad's Rice Pudding

This pudding comes from my dad's attempt to re-create a dish his mother made for him growing up in Mobile, Alabama. Not much of a baker, he makes it for himself every Christmas Eve and learned the hard way that it's delicious if you just follow the recipe.

¾ cup long-grain white rice

2 tablespoons + ½ cup unsalted butter

Dash salt

2 large eggs

1 cup milk

1 cup sugar

2 teaspoons vanilla extract

Preheat the oven to 350°F. Lightly grease a 2-quart casserole dish.

In a saucepan, combine 1½ cups water, rice, 2 tablespoons of the butter, and salt. Bring to a quick boil. Cover, reduce the heat, and simmer for 15 minutes, or until rice has absorbed all liquid.

Stir remaining ½ cup butter into rice until melted.

In a medium bowl, lightly beat eggs. Add milk, sugar, and vanilla and whisk well.

Add milk mixture to rice and stir well. Pour into prepared casserole.

Bake for 15 minutes, or until top is golden brown.

Makes 6 servings

Buttermilk Pound Cake

3 cups sugar

1 cup unsalted butter, softened

5 large eggs

1 tablespoon boiling water

½ teaspoon baking soda

1 cup buttermilk

3 cups sifted all-purpose flour

1 teaspoon lemon extract

1 teaspoon almond extract

Preheat the oven to 350°F. Grease and flour a Bundt pan.

In a large bowl, cream together sugar and butter. Beat in eggs, one at a time.

In a medium bowl, combine boiling water and baking soda. Add buttermilk and stir to combine.

Alternately add flour and buttermilk mixture to butter mixture. Stir in lemon and almond extracts. Mix until well blended.

Pour batter into prepared pan. Bake for 1 hour without opening the oven door; top should be golden.

Let stand for 10 minutes on a cooling rack before unmolding.

Cool to room temperature before slicing.

Makes 10 to 12 servings

Kitchen Note

- You can substitute 2 teaspoons vanilla extract for the lemon and almond extracts.

Mrs. Todd's Angel Food Cake with Lemon Glaze

1¼ cups sifted cake flour

1¾ cups granulated sugar

1¾ cups egg whites (12 to 14 whites),
at room temperature

1½ teaspoons cream of tartar

½ teaspoon salt

1 teaspoon vanilla extract

1 teaspoon almond extract

1 cup confectioners' sugar

3½ tablespoons fresh lemon juice

Sliced strawberries for garnish (optional)

Preheat the oven to 375°F.

Sift flour with ¾ cup of the granulated sugar. Sift 2 more times. Set aside.

In a very clean bowl, beat egg whites, cream of tartar, and salt with an electric mixer at medium speed just until soft peaks form when beater is slowly raised. Do not overbeat.

At high speed, gradually beat in remaining 1 cup granulated sugar, ¼ cup at a time, beating well after each addition. Continue beating until stiff peaks form when beater is slowly raised.

With a rubber spatula, gently fold vanilla and almond extracts into whites.

Sprinkle one-fourth of flour mixture over egg whites. With wire whisk, using an under-and-over motion, gently fold flour mixture into whites (about 15 strokes, rotating the bowl a quarter turn after each stroke). Repeat, one-fourth at a time, with remaining flour.

With rubber spatula, gently scrape batter into an ungreased 10-inch tube pan. With a knife, cut through batter twice to remove any air bubbles. Smooth the top.

Bake on the lowest rack in the oven for 30 to 35 minutes, or until top springs back when gently pressed with finger.

Invert the pan over the neck of a bottle to cool completely, about 2 hours.

Run a knife around the inside of the tube pan and turn out cake.

Mix confectioners' sugar and lemon juice. Drizzle glaze over cooled cake and garnish with strawberries, if you like.

Makes 10 to 12 servings

Kitchen Note

- For good volume, separate eggs while still cold from refrigerator. Then measure out and transfer to a large bowl of an electric mixer and let warm to room temperature, about 1 hour.

Devil's Food Cake with Mocha Frosting

Cake

2 cups granulated sugar

1 cup shortening

5 large eggs

2 cups sifted all-purpose flour

¾ cup unsweetened cocoa powder

¼ teaspoon salt

1 teaspoon baking soda

1 cup buttermilk

½ teaspoon vanilla extract

Chocolate Filling

1 square (1 ounce) semisweet chocolate

1 cup milk

½ cup granulated sugar

2 tablespoons all-purpose flour

1 tablespoon cornstarch

¼ teaspoon salt

2 tablespoons unsalted butter

½ teaspoon vanilla extract

Mocha Frosting

½ cup unsalted butter, softened

1 (1-pound) box confectioners' sugar

3 tablespoons unsweetened cocoa powder

2 teaspoons vanilla extract

3 tablespoons strong coffee, more or less, to get to spreading consistency

½ to 1 cup chopped pecans

To make cake: Preheat the oven to 350°F. Grease and flour two 8-inch cake pans.

In a large bowl, cream together granulated sugar and shortening. Add eggs, one at a time, beating well after each addition.

In a medium bowl, sift together flour, cocoa, and salt.

In a small bowl, mix baking soda into buttermilk.

Alternately add flour mixture and buttermilk to batter a little at a time, until blended. Stir in vanilla.

Divide batter between prepared pans. Bake for 25 to 30 minutes, or until a toothpick inserted in the center comes out clean.

Let cakes cool in pans, then remove from pans to a wire rack to cool.

To make filling: Melt chocolate in top of double boiler over simmering water. Add milk and continue heating.

In a small bowl, mix together granulated sugar, flour, cornstarch,

Kitchen Note

- Be sure to sift the flour for the cake before measuring.

and salt. Add to hot milk mixture, stirring constantly. Cook, stirring, until mixture thickens.

Remove the top from the double boiler and stir in butter and vanilla. Let cool.

To make frosting: In a large bowl, cream together butter and confectioners' sugar. Add cocoa and vanilla. Add coffee by the tablespoon, until frosting is spreading consistency.

To assemble cake: When cake is cool, place one of the cakes bottom side up on a cake plate. Spread the filling over the cake and top with the other cake.

Spread frosting on top and sides of cake and cover top with crushed pecans.

Makes 10 servings

Cocoons

You will need to bake the cocoons in two batches. Wrap half the dough and refrigerate while the first batch bakes.

½ cup + 2 tablespoons unsalted butter, softened

4 heaping tablespoons confectioners' sugar, plus more for finishing cookies

1 tablespoon vanilla extract

1 tablespoon ice water

2 cups cake flour

2 cups pecans, chopped

Preheat the oven to 250°F.

In a large bowl, cream together butter, sugar, vanilla, and ice water.

Toss together flour and pecans in another large bowl, then blend into butter mixture. (This is easiest done with clean hands, as you will also form the cocoons with your hands.)

Once the dough is blended, divide in half and refrigerate half. Form dough into cocoon shapes using about 2 teaspoons of dough for each.

Place on two ungreased baking sheets. Bake for 50 to 60 minutes, or until cooked through. Do not let brown.

Roll cocoons in confectioners' sugar while still hot. Handle with care so they do not break.

Repeat to shape and bake remaining dough.

Makes 4 dozen cocoons

Chocolate Chip Crumb Cake

½ cup unsalted butter, softened

1½ cups sugar

1 cup sour cream

2 large eggs

1 teaspoon vanilla extract

2 cups all-purpose flour

1½ teaspoons baking powder

1 teaspoon baking soda

1½ cups chocolate chips

1 teaspoon ground cinnamon

Preheat the oven to 350°F. Grease a 9- by 13-inch baking pan.

In a large bowl, cream together butter and 1 cup of the sugar. Add sour cream, eggs, and vanilla. Mix well.

In a medium bowl, sift together flour, baking powder, and baking soda.

Add flour mixture to batter and beat until well blended.

In a separate bowl, mix chocolate chips, cinnamon, and remaining ½ cup sugar to make topping.

Pour half of the batter into the prepared pan. Sprinkle half of the topping over the batter. Pour remaining batter over topping. Sprinkle remaining topping on top of batter.

Bake for 25 to 30 minutes, or until golden.

Makes 10 to 12 servings

Kitchen Note

- This is also good as a breakfast coffee cake.

Big's Rum Cake

This recipe is from my friend Dr. Ruth Fredricks's father, James Kellum, who is known by his grandchildren as "Big." He is 91 years young and makes this recipe once a month for our book group.

Cake

- 1 cup chopped pecans or walnuts
- 1 (18.25-ounce) box yellow cake mix
- 1 (5.1-ounce) box JELL-O Instant Vanilla Pudding & Pie Filling
- 4 large eggs
- ½ cup cold water
- ½ cup dark rum
- ½ cup vegetable oil

Glaze

- ½ cup unsalted butter
- 1 cup granulated sugar
- 2 ounces water
- ¼ cup + 2 tablespoons dark rum

Preheat the oven to 325°F. Grease and flour a Bundt pan.

Sprinkle nuts over the bottom of the pan.

To make cake: Mix all remaining cake ingredients in a large bowl and pour batter over nuts in the prepared pan.

Bake for 1 hour, or until a tester inserted in the center comes out clean. Remove from the oven and let cool for half an hour in the pan. When cool, invert to remove cake from pan and place cake on a cake plate.

To make glaze: Melt butter in a small saucepan over medium heat. Stir in sugar and water and bring to a boil. Reduce the heat to medium and boil for 5 minutes, stirring constantly. Remove from the stove and continue to stir constantly while adding rum.

Prick the cake with an ice pick (or a fork) and spoon the glaze over the top and sides. Keep coating with glaze until all the glaze has been absorbed.

Makes 10 to 12 servings

Award-Winning Icebox Cookies

This recipe was given to me by my niece's mother-in-law, Robyn Foral. She entered it in a 4-H club contest many, many years ago and won a purple ribbon.

2 cups firmly packed brown sugar

1 cup unsalted butter, softened

2 large eggs, beaten

4 cups all-purpose flour

1½ teaspoons baking powder

1 teaspoon baking soda

1½ teaspoons maple flavoring

1 cup chopped pecans

In a large bowl, cream together butter and sugar. Add eggs and mix well.

Add flour, baking powder, baking soda, and maple flavoring. Mix well.

Stir in pecans.

Roll dough into a log (2 to 3 inches in diameter) and wrap in wax paper. Refrigerate overnight.

When ready to make the cookies, preheat the oven to 350°F.

Slice log into 36 (¼-inch-thick) rounds and place on 2 ungreased baking sheets or 2 baking sheets lined with parchment paper.

Bake for 9 to 11 minutes, or until lightly browned.

Makes 3 dozen cookies

Kitchen Note

- The wrapped log of dough may also be frozen, then sliced and baked as needed.

Suzy's Monster Cookies

This recipe is from my niece Suzy. It's one of her favorites.

1⅓ cups extra chunky peanut butter

1 cup granulated sugar

1 cup + 2 tablespoons firmly packed brown sugar

½ cup margarine, softened

3 large eggs

2 teaspoons baking soda

1 teaspoon vanilla extract

4½ cups old-fashioned oats

1½ cups M&Ms, butterscotch or chocolate chips, or chopped peanuts

Preheat the oven to 350°F.

In a large bowl, cream together peanut butter, granulated sugar, brown sugar, margarine, eggs, baking soda, and vanilla with an electric mixer on high speed.

Mix in oats and candy by hand.

Drop by tablespoonfuls, about 2 inches apart, onto ungreased baking sheets.

Bake for 12 to 15 minutes, or until lightly browned.

Makes 3 dozen cookies

Kitchen Notes

- I usually use old-fashioned rolled oats, which give the cookie more of an oatmeal/grainy texture than quick-cooking oats.

- I have always used M&Ms because of the color they add—and the kids like them.

Mary Lee's Snickerdoodles

I've always thought that sharing a recipe is "good karma." If you give away one, chances are that you'll get a great recipe in return. My sister-in-law Mary Lee has been making Snickerdoodles since I've known her. Many years ago when I was in college, she graciously sent me this recipe, along with one for Tasty Toffee Treats (opposite), to make for a sorority function. When Mary Lee lost her home along with all of her recipes in Hurricane Katrina, I was so happy to be able to return these recipes to her.

1 cup shortening	2 teaspoons cream of tartar
1½ cups + 2 tablespoons sugar	1 teaspoon baking soda
2 large eggs	½ teaspoon salt
2¾ cups all-purpose flour	2 tablespoons ground cinnamon

Preheat the oven to 400°F.

In a large bowl, combine shortening, 1½ cups of sugar, and eggs and mix thoroughly.

In another large bowl, sift flour, cream of tartar, baking soda, and salt together. Add to shortening mixture and blend until combined. Cover and refrigerate for 30 minutes.

Combine cinnamon and remaining 2 tablespoons sugar on a plate.

Roll dough into balls the size of small walnuts.

Roll dough balls in the cinnamon sugar and place about 2 inches apart on ungreased baking sheets.

Bake for 8 to 10 minutes, or until lightly brown but still soft.

Makes 3 to 4 dozen cookies

Tasty Toffee Treats

1 cup unsalted butter + 1 tablespoon for pan

About 36 salted saltine crackers

1 cup firmly packed dark brown sugar

½ teaspoon vanilla extract

2 cups milk chocolate chips

¾ cup chopped pecans

Preheat the oven to 350°F. Line a jelly-roll pan with foil and lightly coat the foil with 1 tablespoon of the butter.

Arrange crackers in the pan in a single layer with sides touching.

In a saucepan, combine remaining 1 cup butter, the brown sugar, and vanilla. Bring to a boil over medium heat, stirring constantly. Boil 3 to 4 minutes.

Pour hot mixture over crackers and spread evenly.

Bake for 3 to 5 minutes, or until bubbly.

Immediately sprinkle chocolate chips all over, spreading to cover as they melt. Sprinkle with pecans and press lightly.

Refrigerate for 30 minutes, or until set.

Break into roughly 36 pieces and store in a covered container in the refrigerator.

Makes 3 dozen treats

Kitchen Note

- Saltine crackers make the toffee much lighter and crispier than graham crackers. This is a hit with teenagers! You can of course use graham crackers, if you prefer.

Kierstin and Kali's
Chocolate–Peanut Butter Balls

Kierstin and Kali Ruppert, two students from my cooking class at Camp Blackberry, gave me this recipe and said they loved to make it for neighbor and teacher gifts at Christmas.

2 cups cornflakes

2 cups dry milk powder

2 cups creamy peanut butter

2 cups confectioners' sugar

½ cup unsalted butter, melted

15 ounces good-quality semisweet or bittersweet chocolate, chopped

Line a baking sheet or a large metal tray with foil.

Combine cornflakes, milk powder, peanut butter, and sugar in a large bowl. Mix in butter.

Moisten your hands and roll tablespoons of the mixture into balls. Place close together on the prepared baking sheet (they should all fit on one sheet).

Cover the baking sheet and refrigerate overnight.

Line an additional baking sheet with foil.

Melt chocolate in a double boiler over simmering water, stirring occasionally. Remove the top of the double boiler from over water.

Using a fork, dip peanut butter balls, one at a time, into chocolate and transfer to the prepared baking sheet. Refrigerate until chocolate is firm.

Store in an airtight container in the refrigerator for up to 1 week or freeze for up to 1 month. (Soften slightly at room temperature before serving.)

Makes 3 dozen balls

Kitchen Note

- Be sure to use a good-quality chocolate–Kierstin and Kali use Lindt.

How to Make Do
When You Have To

My family was deeply affected by Hurricane Katrina. We lost the century-old family home in Pass Christian, Mississippi, where 37 summers and many of the shared life experiences of our big family took place. My brother Todd's home was so severely damaged it was uninhabitable, and brother Ben lost everything. It was just gone. When the wind and the water subsided, there was only a concrete slab left behind.

Ben has always been the most laid-back of my five siblings, and no matter how dire the circumstance he always finds a bright spot. Ben loves people and they are drawn to him. Maybe it's because he finds his joy in the simple blessings of family, good winds to sail his boat, or a beautiful sunrise to share with his dog. He is my inspiration for "making do when you have to."

The Gathering Place: *For 40 years, family and friends gathered on the porches to feel the Gulf breeze. On Sundays, we laid colorful quilts on the lawn under the oaks for lunch and the occasional nap. Around the kitchen table, the lively banter of three generations peeling boiled shrimp and cracking crabs drowned out the drone of the ceiling fan. The wind and the water destroyed our home . . . but memories . . . well, they last forever.*

In the days following Hurricane Katrina, those of us who lived in Jackson, 3 hours away from the devastation of the storm, would load a pickup truck with supplies and head to Pass Christian to dig through the rubble. My job was to shop for food and supplies. Every night on the long drive home, my sister, Carol, would call me with a list. I would go to the market for food and scour the stores for precious supplies, then help load the truck for the return trip at the crack of dawn. Our town of Pass Christian was 95 percent gone and with few houses left, my brother Ben and his friends found shelter with Chuck and Amy Wood, whose home was spared the devastation. At one time, there were about 30 of them making camp in the Woods' home. Since there was no water or electricity, we would make ice chests full of sandwiches and platters of brownies to feed the motley crew that used the Woods' home as their base camp.

To break up the monotony of sandwiches, one morning I called Ben to tell him I was sending a beef tenderloin. His reaction took me by surprise. He said, "That's great, but don't cook it." I was puzzled by his comment, and he went on to say, "That's something we can do. We can build a fire and cook it."

After a day of backbreaking work, digging through rubble, trying to find even the smallest of possessions, he and his friends would gather on the slab that had once been his home and cook over a fire. When he told me this, I knew he would be okay. In the midst of this enormous tragedy with all their worldly possessions gone, Ben and his friends still had their gathering time. They had each other and they knew "how to make do when you have to."

This book is about gatherings—whether a supper in the kitchen, a tree-trimming party at holiday time, a favorite tea party, or a Deep South brunch. And yes, it's fun to have a theme and pull out all the stops with beautiful dinnerware and linens. The most important thing, however, is taking the time to be together. You may not have beautiful dinnerware and tablecloths; you may not have a table at all. Your gathering may be on a concrete slab after a hurricane, but no matter the circumstance, you can always take time to gather with family and friends.

How to Host
a Successful Gathering

My first parties were small, cozy gatherings where my guests dressed in their Sunday best. These "events" were usually some version of an afternoon tea party, designed to showcase my finest china and accessories. We sipped imaginary teas, enjoyed lively conversation, and feasted on all manner of sweets and tiny sandwiches. The guests were well-mannered, appreciative of my hospitality, and adored whatever I served . . . even Chatty Cathy, the most cantankerous and hard to please of all my dolls.

The make-believe entertaining of my early childhood years grew into real-world experiences as my mother and grandmother nurtured and encouraged my love of hospitality. They graciously included me in the magical rituals of entertaining, whether it was the bridge club, sewing circle, or luncheon club.

According to family lore, soon after I began to walk I was pressed into service passing linen napkins when my grandmother hosted the Pine Burr Club, a gathering of ladies for refreshments and stimulating conversation, in her tiny living room in Hattiesburg, Mississippi. (South Mississippi has a wealth of pine trees, thus the club's name). Passing the dainty embroidered beverage napkins in a silver basket became my signature service as a young helper. From a child's vantage point, I absorbed many of the entertaining principles I later applied to my work as a cooking teacher, caterer, and host.

IT'S ALL ABOUT STYLE

When it comes to having successful parties, my mother, Dorothy Puckett, has been my teacher and my greatest inspiration. She can serve a bowl of cereal on the kitchen counter and make it a memorable experience for her guests. She opens her kitchen cabinet and reaches for a beautiful bowl, a silver spoon, a colorful placemat and napkin, a small crystal pitcher for the milk, and a berry bowl with fresh fruit. When her bathrobed guests enter the kitchen, they start their day with a smile and the unmistakable warmth of a caring host.

Perhaps the most profound lesson I've learned from her is that you don't have to be a great cook to entertain successfully. You don't even have to be a good cook! Great parties can be created with the humblest of foods or artfully assembled from a collection of store-bought provisions. Fun and fellowship make the party, not slaving away in the kitchen for days on end. As a host, time is better spent creating a festive atmosphere and planning for the enjoyment of your guests.

With her style and intuitive expertise as a host, my mother has coached me through many an entertaining crisis. Years ago when my sister, Carol, was working in the Midwest, she decided to treat her new friends to a Southern Sunday brunch. Her Midwestern friends were fascinated by her Southern ways, and Carol decided it was time to satisfy their curiosity about the Southern table. The cheese grits, buttermilk biscuits, and shrimp Creole were made ahead. The milk punch was chilling in the refrigerator awaiting the necessary bourbon. The only thing left was to fry the chicken, a signature Southern Sunday dish Carol had unfortunately never made before.

The shriveled and blackened results of her heroic efforts looked nothing like the crisp golden brown delicacies that came out of our grandmother's iron skillet. Not to mention that Carol almost burned down her house. A frantic call to Mom saved the day. My mother swore that she had never personally fried a chicken in her whole life (even though grandmother was a pro) and she couldn't believe Carol would even attempt it. Less than an hour before the party, she sent her speeding off to the nearest no-name fried chicken restaurant for a large box of chicken. The crisp golden pieces were placed on a beautiful platter and the telltale box was consigned to the bottom of the garbage can, lest it be accidentally discovered. When her guests raved about the "Southern" fried chicken, Carol just smiled and said, "I'm so glad you liked it."

PROPER PLANNING MAKES PERFECT PARTIES

Planning ahead is another key to a successful party, and my mother's relaxed demeanor before greeting her guests has been my example. Her philosophy is to be ready an hour before the gathering because you never know what might come up, and you don't want to appear harried and out of breath when your guests arrive. She prefers to be sitting in the front porch swing or in the living room, ready to greet her guests when they arrive. Seeing her at ease instantly relaxes them and creates a welcoming and serene atmosphere.

Mom tells the story of arriving on time for a friend's fine dinner party. The husband of the hostess greeted them at the door, but the hostess was mysteriously absent. After 45 minutes of polite conversation among the waiting guests, the hostess dramatically descended the stairs, remarking that she had been "fixing her hair!" For my parties, I prefer to start the cooking, get dressed and ready, and then come back and finish in the kitchen. I enlist my teenage son to help with last-minute details, light the candles, or put the dogs in their kennels. My hair would never keep me away from my guests.

Keep in mind that good parties don't have to be complicated. When I decide to have a gathering, I immediately begin planning my menu. Some gatherings are organized around holidays or special occasions like birthdays or football games, but many times I'll find a recipe in a cookbook or magazine that I want to make and decide to invite friends so I can try it out on them.

Whatever the occasion, I shop for groceries 2 days before the party and prep most of the food the day before. The night before my guests arrive, I set the table, polish the silver, and arrange my flowers—giving them time to open on the day of the party. I leave very little to do on the day of the gathering, so I'm relaxed and can enjoy my guests so much more.

Over the years I've learned what works and what doesn't for my home and my abilities. Casual dinner parties and kitchen suppers—where some of the food can be made ahead—work best for me. I am a single parent and, as both host and cook, I enjoy having my guests in the kitchen with me as I prepare the food. I certainly don't want to miss the party, and I've learned that guests enjoy participating, so I gladly turn over a task or two.

GUESS WHO'S COMING TO DINNER?

Guests can make or break the success of any gathering, so planning the guest list requires as much forethought as planning the food. Beware of trying to accommodate too many people. A small party is no time for repaying social obligations and you should have a firm number in mind. Decide how many your table or entertaining space will comfortably hold and stick to it. Guests feel more special if they are comfortable and not crowded. I always start with a list of people I enjoy and then think about who would be interesting and compatible. I invite interesting people . . . not just couples . . . and enjoy mixing up guests from my various worlds—church, school, neighbors, career.

For seated parties, place cards can be a hostess's best friend. Thinking through your seating beforehand ensures that conversation flows. Taking the guesswork out of seating also contributes to the comfort and enjoyment of the guests and insures that the host or hostess will have easy access to the kitchen.

The invitation—whether printed, e-mailed, or telephoned—should tell the story of the party. In addition to setting the date and time, a proper invitation should also set the tone and clue-in guests on how to dress and what to expect. I'm a big fan of the printed invitation, whether it's a sit-down dinner for eight or a casual picnic for a crowd in the backyard. It serves as a tangible reminder to the guests and cuts down on the kind of misinformation that can easily be transmitted by phone or voice mail. Another personal preference is to place invitations in an envelope and address them by hand, even though the invitation may be printed on a card. A hand-addressed envelope adds to the importance of the invitation and, with the addition of a colorful clever stamp, helps it to stand out in the sea of catalogs, bills, and junk mail.

TIME IS NOT ON MY SIDE

I enjoy entertaining on a moment's notice, so I always keep a few basics on hand. I've hosted many a drop-in guest or an impromptu party with my stash of cute cocktail napkins, good wine, and cheese and crackers. I usually have everything I need for Clara's Corn Dip (page 97) and Hot Artichoke Parmesan Dip (page 133), so while guests enjoy these tasty appetizers, I turn my attention to the other preparations. With three dogs and teenager, I really try to keep our house relatively tidy because I never want to tell friends they can't come to my home because it's a mess.

Outdoor entertaining is especially well-suited to last-minute gatherings, if you cover the basics. The grill should always be cleaned after each use, and you should have charcoal or filled butane bottles on hand so you're ready to go on a moment's notice. The patio, deck, or yard, if you have one, should be regularly maintained so a party doesn't spawn another big cleaning project. Stock a seasonal supply of paper products, along with acrylic, plastic, or metal buckets for beverages. Most important, the food for dining al fresco should be easy to prepare. Everyone loves the taste of hamburgers, hot dogs, chicken, steak, or fish cooked outdoors—so keep the main dish simple and add easy sides as well. Pick-up desserts like cookies and brownies (see pages 28–29, 58, 85, 128–129, 172–173, and 206–210) are always appreciated, but I've discovered that a passed basket or tray of ice cream sandwiches is a popular end to any outdoor party. I buy a variety of ice cream sandwiches or I make my own (page 149). Guests love to riffle through the basket and discover their favorite flavors.

MAKING IT FUN

Adding an element of the unexpected lightens up any gathering and is a great way for guests to get into the party spirit. At a luncheon I attended celebrating a friend's second (or was it third?) wedding, guests were invited to wear old bridesmaid's dresses. You can just imagine the parade of outfits stretching back 30 years . . . most of which could be zipped only halfway up the back or side. There were red velvet empire-waist dresses trimmed in lace, and frilly Southern belle hoopskirts that would make Scarlett O'Hara envious. The party was immediately lifted to another level as guests gathered at the front door to watch other partygoers enter in their wedding regalia.

Or here's another fun idea. Hats. Putting a hat on everyone's head can transform an ordinary party into a festive fashion event. One of my sister's luncheon invitations asked her guests to "please wear a hat." When the guests arrived, there were baseball caps, mink pillboxes from the 1950s, and dramatic wide-brimmed flowered hats not seen outside of the Kentucky Derby or English horse races.

The outdoors, too, offers a wide range of opportunities to add the unexpected. Torches, lanterns, and lawn games are just a few possibilities. At a recent poolside cookout for a group of friends, we decided to pass a colorful array of water pistols on the dessert tray. No doubt about it, water pistols are guaranteed to turn grown men (and women) into 5-year-olds, and this group turned a sedate poolside dinner into pandemonium. Casual attire was quickly borrowed and madness ensued when the guests jumped into the pool. It was certainly a memorable party that will not be forgotten soon.

IT'S ALL ABOUT YOU!

In the end, a successful gathering is a reflection of your style and unique personality. Guests are always drawn to the authentic, and most times they would rather eat from a pot of chili on the kitchen stove than know you exhausted yourself making some exotic dish. If the hospitality is warm and sincere, that's the memory they'll take home.

To be a successful entertainer, you simply have to be yourself. One of life's biggest lessons for me was discovering, like Dorothy in the Wizard of Oz, that home is in our hearts. And wherever I've lived, I've taken my Mississippi home with me. I learned early on that it was pointless and false to try to change myself . . . and my entertaining . . . to match my surroundings. I have confidently served cheese grits, my grandmother's dinner rolls, and buttermilk pound cake in Dallas, Miami, and Palos Verdes, California, to a wonderful range of friends and family who all loved every bite.

And that's successful entertaining.

Index

Underscored page references indicate sidebars. **Boldface** references indicate photographs.

Authors' Bios

Helen Puckett DeFrance was born and raised in Jackson, Mississippi. The fourth child in a family of six children, she learned cooking from her grandmother Helen Todd. Helen combined a passion for cooking with an unparalleled gift for teaching to create the Camp Blackberry cooking program for kids at the prestigious Blackberry Farm near Knoxville, Tennessee (where she's been a featured guest chef for holiday events since 2002). A graduate of the master's program at Pepperdine University with a specialty in Montessori training (a hands-on, experiential teaching method), she presents her cooking program, THYME to Cook!, in schools across the country, as well as at the Everyday Gourmet in her hometown, Viking Cooking Schools nationwide, and Blackberry Farm, among others. She lives in Jackson with her son, Martin, along with her three dogs, Eddie, Henri, and Lucky.

Carol Puckett, the writer of this book, is president of the Viking Hospitality Group, a division of Viking Range Corporation. She is also the founder of the Everyday Gourmet, a Jackson-based cooking store and cooking school, and owner of a companion store, the Everyday Gardener. She serves on the board of directors of the International Ballet Competition, the Southern Food and Beverage Museum, the Southern Foodways Alliance, and the Center for the Study of Southern Culture. When not cooking, eating, writing, or talking about food, she enjoys hiking, fishing, canoeing, and living the life of a Sweet Potato Queen.

For more information on At Home Café, go to www.athomecafe.net.

Conversion Chart

These equivalents have been slightly rounded to make measuring easier.

VOLUME MEASUREMENTS

U.S.	Imperial	Metric
¼ tsp	–	1 ml
½ tsp	–	2 ml
1 tsp	–	5 ml
1 Tbsp	–	15 ml
2 Tbsp (1 oz)	1 fl oz	30 ml
¼ cup (2 oz)	2 fl oz	60 ml
⅓ cup (3 oz)	3 fl oz	80 ml
½ cup (4 oz)	4 fl oz	120 ml
⅔ cup (5 oz)	5 fl oz	160 ml
¾ cup (6 oz)	6 fl oz	180 ml
1 cup (8 oz)	8 fl oz	240 ml

WEIGHT MEASUREMENTS

U.S.	Metric
1 oz	30 g
2 oz	60 g
4 oz (¼ lb)	115 g
5 oz (⅓ lb)	145 g
6 oz	170 g
7 oz	200 g
8 oz (½ lb)	230 g
10 oz	285 g
12 oz (¾ lb)	340 g
14 oz	400 g
16 oz (1 lb)	455 g
2.2 lb	1 kg

LENGTH MEASUREMENTS

U.S.	Metric
¼"	0.6 cm
½"	1.25 cm
1"	2.5 cm
2"	5 cm
4"	11 cm
6"	15 cm
8"	20 cm
10"	25 cm
12" (1')	30 cm

PAN SIZES

U.S.	Metric
8" cake pan	20 × 4 cm sandwich or cake tin
9" cake pan	23 × 3.5 cm sandwich or cake tin
11" × 7" baking pan	28 × 18 cm baking tin
13" × 9" baking pan	32.5 × 23 cm baking tin
15" × 10" baking pan	38 × 25.5 cm baking tin (Swiss roll tin)
1½ qt baking dish	1.5 liter baking dish
2 qt baking dish	2 liter baking dish
2 qt rectangular baking dish	30 × 19 cm baking dish
9" pie plate	22 × 4 or 23 × 4 cm pie plate
7" or 8" springform pan	18 or 20 cm springform or loose-bottom cake tin
9" × 5" loaf pan	23 × 13 cm or 2 lb narrow loaf tin or pâté tin

TEMPERATURES

Fahrenheit	Centigrade	Gas
140°	60°	–
160°	70°	–
180°	80°	–
225°	105°	¼
250°	120°	½
275°	135°	1
300°	150°	2
325°	160°	3
350°	180°	4
375°	190°	5
400°	200°	6
425°	220°	7
450°	230°	8
475°	245°	9
500°	260°	–